passion
seductive food

Published by Murdoch Books®, a division of Murdoch Magazines Pty Ltd.

Murdoch Books® Australia
GPO Box 1203
Sydney NSW 1045
Phone: + 61 (0) 2 4352 7000
Fax: + 61 (0) 2 4352 7026

Murdoch Books UK Limited
Ferry House
51–57 Lacy Road
Putney, London SW15 1PR
Phone: + 44 (0) 20 8355 1480
Fax: + 44 (0) 20 8355 1499

Design Concept: Marylouise Brammer
Designer: Michelle Cutler
Recipe introductions: Lucy Campbell
Editorial Director: Diana Hill
Editor: Zoë Harpham
Food Director: Lulu Grimes
Recipes developed by the Murdoch Books Test Kitchen.

Chief Executive: Juliet Rogers
Publisher: Kay Scarlett
Production Manager: Kylie Kirkwood

National Library of Australia Cataloguing-in-Publication Data
Passion. Includes index. ISBN 1 74045 039 6 1. Cookery. 641.5.

PRINTED IN CHINA by Toppan Printing Co. (HK) Ltd.
Printed 2002.

IMPORTANT: Those who might be at risk from the effects of salmonella food poisoning (the elderly, pregnant
women, young children and those suffering from immune deficiency diseases) should consult their GP with any
concerns about eating raw eggs.

passion
seductive food

MURDOCH
B O O K S

contents

passion

licky, sticky and yummy

Some foods are popular because they seduce us with their fragrance and flavour; others because they evoke memories of childhood. And still others because they are classics that can't be improved upon. This book is full of favourite foods, from sweet desserts remembered from childhood to spicy dishes that have worked their magic on us as adults. We've decided to link these recipes by food type, be that sexy, spicy, steamy, creamy, salty or sugary.

Simply got to have a luscious dessert? Go straight to the Sugary chapter. Craving something a little savoury? Generously salted fish and chips or a perfect cheese board will satisfy — both found in the Salty chapter. In the middle of winter, you might delve into the Steamy chapter, with its selection of melt-in-the-mouth pies, slowly cooked casseroles and seriously comforting desserts. But at the height of summer, you might prefer something fresh and crisp with a bit of bite like Thai beef salad from the Spicy chapter. And sometimes you need something silky and creamy, perhaps Spaghetti carbonara or a decadent Chocolate mousse, both found in the Creamy chapter. Then there's sexy food, which includes food that sets the scene for seduction or seals an established relationship.

So let yourself be seduced by the food you love to eat.

sexy
sensuous meals for two

The icy perfection of a classic martini sets the tone for the most elegant of evenings.

martini

ice cubes	Half-fill a mixing glass with ice. Pour in
45 ml (1¹/₂ fl oz) gin	the gin and vermouth, then stir. Strain into
15 ml (¹/₂ fl oz) dry vermouth	a chilled martini glass and garnish with a
(or to taste)	green olive.
green olive	Serves 1.

The Cosmopolitan is a drink to be consumed in your best designer outfit.

cosmopolitan

ice cubes
30 ml (1 fl oz) citrus-flavoured vodka
15 ml (1/2 fl oz) Cointreau
45 ml (1 1/2 fl oz) cranberry juice
10 ml (1/4 fl oz) lime juice
lime twist

Half-fill a cocktail shaker with ice. Pour in the vodka, Cointreau, cranberry juice and lime juice and shake well. Strain into a large, chilled martini glass. Garnish with a twist of lime.
Serves 1.

Asparagus and egg are a great team, and the choice of pretty, delicate quail eggs to accompany the slender spears is an inspired one.

asparagus with quail eggs and lime hollandaise

2 tbs virgin olive oil
16 asparagus spears, trimmed
1 tsp white vinegar
6 quail eggs
2 egg yolks
150 g (5½ oz) butter, melted
2 tbs lime juice
a sprinkle of paprika
good-quality Parmesan cheese shavings

Using half the oil as a kind of thin glue, coat the asparagus in 1 teaspoon black pepper.

Half-fill a deep frying pan with water and bring to a gentle simmer, then splash in the vinegar — this will stop the egg white separating from the yolk as it cooks. Crack each quail egg, one at a time, into a small bowl before gently sliding it into the pan. Cook until the egg white turns opaque, then carefully remove from the pan with a spatula and keep warm.

Heat the remaining oil in a large frying pan and cook the asparagus over high heat until tender and bright green, about 2 minutes.

To make the hollandaise, whizz the egg yolks in a blender and slowly add the melted butter in a thin, steady stream. Mix until all the butter has been added and you have a thick, creamy sauce. Stir in the lime juice, then taste a little and add salt and pepper if it needs it.

Divide the asparagus between two warmed plates, top with three quail eggs per person, drizzle with hollandaise and sprinkle with paprika and Parmesan cheese shavings. Best served immediately.
Serves 2 as a starter.

artichokes vinaigrette

2 globe artichokes
juice of half a lemon

For the vinaigrette:
2$\frac{1}{2}$ tbs olive oil
1 spring onion (scallion), finely chopped
1 tbs white wine
1 tbs white wine vinegar
$\frac{1}{4}$ tsp Dijon mustard
pinch of sugar
2 tsp finely chopped parsley

Break the stalks from the artichokes, pulling out any strings at the same time, and then trim the bases flat. Boil the artichokes in a large pan of salted, lemony water. You'll need a small plate on top of them to keep them submerged. Simmer until a leaf from the base comes away easily, about half an hour. Cool under running water, then drain upside down.

To make the vinaigrette, heat 1 tablespoon of the oil in a small saucepan, add the spring onion and cook over low heat for 2 minutes. Cool a little, then add the wine, vinegar, mustard and sugar and slowly whisk in the rest of the oil. Season, then add half the parsley.

Sit an artichoke on each plate and gently prise it open a little. Spoon on some dressing, letting it drizzle into the artichoke and around the plate. Pour the rest of the dressing into a small bowl. Sprinkle each artichoke with parsley.

Eat the leaves one by one, dipping them in the vinaigrette and scraping the flesh off the leaves between your teeth. When you reach the middle, pull off any tiny leaves and then use a teaspoon to remove the furry choke. Now you can eat the tender base or 'heart'. Serves 2 as a starter.

Dipping each succulent leaf into the tart vinaigrette and slowly sucking the delicious flavours can be quite a turn on. Are you prepared?

This is such an elegant soup that you should keep it specially for those you aim to impress.

crab bisque

500 g (1 lb 2 oz) live crabs
25 g (1 oz) butter
quarter of a carrot, finely chopped
quarter of an onion, finely chopped
half a celery stalk, finely chopped
1 bay leaf
1 sprig of thyme
1 tbs tomato purée
1 tbs brandy
4 tbs dry white wine
500 ml (2 cups) fish stock
1½ tbs rice
1½ tbs thick (double/heavy) cream
pinch of cayenne pepper

To kill the crabs humanely, freeze them for 1 hour. Remove the top shell and bony tail flap from the underside of each crab, then remove the gills from both sides of the crab and the grit sac. Detach the claws and legs.

Heat the butter in a large saucepan. Add the vegetables, bay leaf and thyme and cook over medium heat for 3 minutes, but don't let the vegetables colour. Add the crab claws, legs and body and cook until the shells turn red, about 5 minutes. Add the tomato purée, brandy and wine and simmer until reduced by half.

Pour in the stock and 250 ml (1 cup) water and bring to the boil, then reduce to a simmer for 5 minutes. Remove the shells and reserve the claws. Finely crush the shells in a food processor with a little of the soup. Return the crushed shells to the soup with the rice. Bring to the boil, reduce the heat, cover the pan and simmer until the rice is very soft, half an hour.

Strain into a clean pan through a fine sieve lined with damp muslin, pressing down firmly to extract all the cooking liquid. Stir in the cream and season with salt and cayenne, then gently reheat. Serve garnished with the claws. Serves 2 as a starter.

simply dressed scallops

12 scallops on their shells
2 French shallots, finely chopped
100 ml (3$^1/_2$ fl oz) verjuice
85 g (3 oz) butter, chilled and cut into
1 cm ($^1/_2$ inch) cubes
1 Roma (plum) tomato, finely chopped
2 spring onions (scallions), green part only,
thinly sliced
2 tbs extra virgin olive oil

Start by preparing the scallops — discard the roe and black muscle, then remove the scallops from their shells. Rinse and dry the shells and set aside because you'll be using them to serve.

Now for the dressing. Put the shallots and verjuice in a small saucepan and bring to the boil. Cook until reduced by a third, about 2 minutes. Take the pan off the hob, then whisk in the butter, a cube at a time. Stir in the tomato and spring onions and season generously with salt and pepper.

Scallops only need to be cooked very briefly over high heat — fry them in olive oil for about 1 minute on each side. Return the scallops to their shells, then drizzle them with the fragrant buttery dressing.
Serves 2 as a starter.

Scallops have a fresh taste of the sea that is best enjoyed when served with the simplest of dressings.

The small but perfectly formed spheres of caviar deserve special treatment. Use a mother-of-pearl spoon, as silver will give the caviar a metallic taste. Also, mother-of-pearl is less likely to break the delicate eggs.

classic blini

200 g (7 oz) buckwheat flour
125 g (1 cup) plain (all-purpose) flour
2 tsp dried yeast
625 ml (2½ cups) warm milk
2 tbs melted butter
3 eggs, separated
caviar or salmon roe
sour cream

Sift the buckwheat and plain flours into a large non-metallic bowl. Add the yeast and ½ teaspoon salt and mix. Make a well in the centre and pour in the warm milk. Mix to a batter and beat for a couple of minutes to get rid of any lumps. Cover the bowl and leave to rise for an hour or two, by which stage you should have a bubbly batter.

Now beat the bubbles out of the batter. Add the melted butter and 3 egg yolks and beat them in. In a separate bowl, whisk the 3 egg whites to a mound of stiff peaks, then fold these into the batter. Leave alone for another 10 minutes.

Grease a heavy-based frying pan (or even better, a blini pan) with butter and fry spoonfuls of the batter until bubbles rise to the surface and the underneath browns. Flip the blini over and cook the other side until brown, about a minute. Keep warm in the oven until you are ready to serve them with caviar and sour cream. Unless you're planning on an evening feasting solely on blini, you probably won't get through them all. Freeze any leftovers, then gently reheat on another occasion.
Makes about 40.

succulent oysters

A platter of oysters is a wonderful way to start a meal, particularly because they are so easy to prepare, but make such a great impression. Start with fresh ones on the shell and see if their aphrodisiac reputation is deserved. You can either serve them natural with just a squeeze of lemon juice, or make one or two of the dressings on the opposite page. Each of the dressings is enough for a dozen oysters. Depending on how much you like oysters, anywhere from a dozen to two dozen will be ample for two people. If you have a good fishmonger, you may be able to buy oysters from different sources — say some Pacific or European oysters and some rock oysters — but it's not necessary. What matters most is that you're buying them fresh. You'll need plenty of rock salt on your serving plates to keep the oysters balanced, and lots of lemon wedges for squeezing. A word of warning — not everyone likes oysters, so before you present the lovingly prepared platter to your guest, it might be worth while finding out their feelings on the matter.

Oyster preparation

Ideally, an oyster should be bought live, with the shell closed. In this state, it should feel heavy and be full of water. If you are buying open oysters, look for plump, moist ones that have creamy flesh with a clear liquid surrounding it. They should smell like the sea and have no shell particles. To check if they are alive, prick the cilla (little hairs around the edge of the flesh): if it retracts, the oyster is alive.

Unopened, oysters can be kept in the fridge for up to 1 week. If opened, store in their liquid and eat within 24 hours. Remove the oysters from the shells, then rinse the shells under cold water. Pat the shells dry and return the oysters to their shells.

If you have to shuck your own oysters, you'll need an oyster shucker to prevent an accident — they have a special guard to protect your hand. First, wrap a tea towel around the unshucked oyster. Next, work the blade of the oyster shucker into the oyster and twist to break the hinge. Now remove the top shell, and slip the shucker between the oyster and the shell to release. Rinse both to remove grit, then replace the oyster.

Tomato and coriander salsa

Cut 2 small vine-ripened tomatoes in half and remove the seeds with a teaspoon. Finely dice the tomato flesh and put in a small bowl with 2 tablespoons finely chopped red onion and 1 tablespoon chopped coriander (cilantro) leaves. Mix together well. Combine 1 tablespoon rice vinegar and 1/2 teaspoon caster sugar in a jug, then stir into the tomato salsa. Season to taste with salt and freshly ground black pepper and refrigerate until ready to serve on the oysters.

Chilli and lime sauce

Heat a teaspoon of peanut oil in a small saucepan, add a crushed garlic clove and cook for a minute, or until softened. Stir in 2 teaspoons lime juice, 1 tablespoon sweet chilli sauce, 1/2 teaspoon sesame oil and 1 teaspoon fish sauce and simmer for a minute, or until just thickened. Allow to cool completely before serving with the oysters.

warm figs in a crispy prosciutto blanket

50 g (1¾ oz) unsalted butter
2 tbs orange juice
12 sage leaves
6 fresh figs, halved lengthways
6 long, thin slices of prosciutto, halved

Gently melt the butter, then cook until the froth subsides and the milk solids appear as brown specks on the bottom of the pan, up to 10 minutes. Strain the butter into a bowl by pouring it through a strainer lined with a clean tea towel or paper towel. Stir the orange juice into the strained butter to impart a delicate citrus flavour.

Sit a sage leaf on each fig half, then use a slice of prosciutto as a belt around the middle of each one, with the ends tucked under the bottom of the fig. Arrange the figs, cut-side up, on a baking tray and brush lightly with the citrusy butter.

Place the baking tray of figs under a hot grill (broiler) and cook the figs until the prosciutto becomes slightly crispy — 1 to 2 minutes should be long enough.
Serves 2 as a starter.

A ripe fig is the most seductive of all fruits, and here they are caressed by a blanket of prosciutto.

A fondue is about more than the food — it's a ritual that gives you a chance to relax with a group of friends, or just one special person. Make sure you've got plenty of wine on hand.

fondue cheese fest

half a garlic clove
1 bottle dry white wine
520 g (4 cups) grated Gruyère cheese
520 g (4 cups) grated Emmental cheese
2 tbs cornflour (cornstarch)
shot of kirsch
pinch of freshly grated nutmeg
cubes of bread

Rub the inside of a fondue pot with the garlic. Pour in the wine and bring it to the boil on the stove. Stir in both the cheeses and the cornflour and melt the cheese slowly, stirring constantly. Fire up the fondue burner and lift on the pot, then stir in the kirsch and grated nutmeg.

Supply a big bowl of bread cubes and some forks, then dip the bread, one cube at a time, into the cheesy goo — make sure your bread cubes aren't too big because double dipping is a definite no-no.
Serves 2–6.

mussels with saffron, lemon grass and tomatoes

750 g (1 lb 10 oz) black mussels
1–2 tbs olive oil
half an onion, finely chopped
3 French shallots, finely chopped
1 stem lemon grass, white part only,
finely chopped
pinch of saffron threads
3 Roma (plum) tomatoes, chopped
125 ml (1/2 cup) dry white wine
1 garlic clove, crushed
1 tsp sugar
1 tbs chopped flat-leaf (Italian) parsley
crusty bread

First of all, prepare the mussels. Scrub them with a stiff brush and remove the hairy beards. Throw away any that have opened or have broken shells.

Heat the oil in a large saucepan and fry the onion, shallots and lemon grass until golden. Add the saffron and tomatoes and cook until the tomatoes start to soften, about 5 minutes. Splash in the wine and 3 tablespoons water and bring to the boil. Now put the lid on and let the broth boil away merrily for about 10 minutes.

Add the mussels to the saucepan and put the lid on again. Now cook the mussels for about 5 minutes, shaking the pan occasionally, until they have opened. Throw away any mussels that haven't opened by now. Stir in the garlic, sugar and parsley and season with salt and freshly ground black pepper. Serve immediately with plenty of crusty bread to soak up the glorious juices.
Serves 2.

Go to your fish markets early for the freshest produce, buy a loaf of bread just out of the oven, then sit back and enjoy plump, juicy mussels in an aromatic broth.

Sweet crab meat whipped into a fluffy, golden soufflé — this is the sort of dish to keep for occasions when you want to show off.

fluffy crab soufflés

15 g (1/2 oz) butter, melted
1 clove pressed into an onion quarter
1 bay leaf
2 black peppercorns
4 tbs milk
2 tsp butter
half a French shallot, finely chopped
2 tsp plain (all-purpose) flour
1 egg yolk
85 g (3 oz) cooked crab meat
pinch of cayenne pepper
3 egg whites

Brush two 125 ml (1/2 cup) ramekins with the melted butter. Put the onion, bay leaf, peppercorns and milk into a small pan. Gently bring to the boil, then take off the hob and leave to infuse for 10 minutes. Now strain it.

Melt the butter in a saucepan, then cook the shallot in it until soft but not browned. Stir in the flour and cook, still stirring, until it turns deep ivory. Take the pan off the heat, then slowly pour in the milk, whisking until smooth. Return to the heat and simmer for 3 minutes, stirring continuously. Beat in the egg yolk. Add the crab meat and stir over the heat until the mixture is hot and thickens again (don't let it boil). Pour into a large heatproof bowl, then add the cayenne and season well.

Whisk the egg whites in a clean, dry bowl until they form soft peaks. Fold a quarter of the egg white into the soufflé mixture, then gently, but thoroughly, fold in the rest. Pour into the ramekins and then run your thumb around the inside rim of each one. Put the ramekins on a baking tray and bake in a 200°C (400°F/Gas 6) oven until you have well risen soufflés that wobble slightly when tapped, about 12 minutes. Serve quickly. Serves 2.

big spinach ravioli pillows

For the filling:
1 tbs butter
half a small onion, finely chopped
40 g (1½ oz) baby spinach leaves
125 g (4½ oz) ricotta
2 tbs double cream

2 fresh lasagne sheets
50 g (1¾ oz) frozen spinach, thawed
125 ml (½ cup) chicken stock

Start with the filling. Fry the onion in the butter until soft, about 5 minutes. Add the spinach and cook for 4 minutes. Take the pan off the hob, cool to room temperature and then chop the spinach. Stir in the ricotta and 1½ tablespoons of the cream, then season.

To make the ravioli, cut out eight 8 cm (3 inch) squares from the lasagne sheets and cook them in a large saucepan of boiling salted water until *al dente*. Drain.

Line a baking tray with baking paper and lay out half the pieces of pasta on the tray. Divide the filling into four portions and spoon into the centre of each square. Top with the other pasta squares and seal them to make little pillows, then cover with a damp tea towel.

To make the sauce, blitz the spinach with a little of the stock in a food processor until smooth. Scoop into a pan with the rest of the stock and heat for 2 minutes. Add the rest of the cream, stir well, season and take the pan off the hob.

Warm the ravioli in a 180°C (350°F/Gas 4) oven. Serve drizzled with sauce. Great with a salad. Serves 2.

Every bite of these luscious parcels is a gift. Give them to someone you love.

Delectable morsels of seafood hiding among slippery strands of spaghetti make for a sexy feast.

spaghetti with sea treasures

pinch of saffron threads
125 ml (1/2 cup) dry white wine
500 g (1 lb 2 oz) clams (vongole)
100 g (31/2 oz) small squid tubes
200 g (7 oz) spaghetti
1–2 garlic cloves, crushed
3 tomatoes, peeled and chopped
2 tbs olive oil
2 baby octopus, cleaned
250 g (9 oz) raw prawns (shrimp),
peeled and deveined
4–5 scallops, cleaned
3 tbs chopped parsley
lemon wedges

Soak the saffron in wine. Scrub the clams clean. Rinse well and discard any that are broken, or open ones that don't close when tapped on a bench. Put them in a large pan with 100 ml (31/2 fl oz) water. Cover and cook over high heat until they open, about 2 minutes. Now throw away any that are still closed. Drain, reserving the precious liquid. Prise the clams from their shells and set aside.

Lay the squid out flat, skin-side up, and score a diamond pattern into the flesh, being careful not to cut all the way through. Slice diagonally into 2 x 4 cm (3/4 x 11/2 inch) strips.

Cook the pasta in a large pot of boiling water until *al dente*. Drain, then return to the pot.

Meanwhile, briefly fry the garlic and tomato in the oil, then pour in the infused wine and the reserved clam liquid. Season and simmer until reduced by half. Add the squid, octopus and prawns and cook until the squid turns opaque. Add the scallops, clam meat and parsley and cook until the scallops turn opaque. Toss most of it through the spaghetti, then scoop onto a platter. Spoon the rest of the sauce on top and serve with lemon wedges. Serves 2.

seafood platter

A seafood platter is easy to prepare and it can be a real feast for two. The great thing about this platter is that you can buy all the seafood pre-cooked from fish markets, fishmongers and sometimes even the fish counter at good supermarkets, so there's not much for you to do.

Crab's sweet meat makes it ideal for a special seafood platter. Depending on how much else you are serving, you can buy one crab per person or share one between the two of you. If you're feeling extravagant, add two lobster halves — lobster is the ultimate indulgence, and there's something particularly sensuous about sharing it between two. See the opposite page for how to deal with lobster and crab like a pro. Add a dozen cooked prawns and some shucked oysters and you have a veritable feast. Round it out with smoked salmon or trout, or whatever else takes your fancy.

Although the actual seafood is the most important element of your platter, don't neglect the presentation if you really want to make an impact. If it's a hot day, chill the platter you'll be using or serve the seafood on a bed of crushed ice. Be sure to provide a lobster pick or long, small fork to extract the precious sweet meat from the claws of lobsters and crabs. Provide plenty of lemon or lime wedges and some tartare sauce to enjoy with your seafood. Set the tone with some candles, then add a couple of finger bowls with some blossoms floating in them for a perfect evening of romance.

Crab

When you're buying cooked crab, make sure they smell fresh and are undamaged and their legs and feet are drawn into the body (if they were dead when cooked, their legs will be looser). To prepare crab, lift the 'apron', the small flap on the underside of the crab, and prise off the top hard shell. Remove the soft internal organs and pull off the spongy grey fingers (the gills). Using a large sharp knife, cut the crab lengthways through the centre of the body, to form two halves with the legs attached. Cut each half of the crab in half again, crossways. Remove the meat with a knife or lobster/crab pick. You can either use the same dressing as for the lobster or try a simple dressing of soy sauce mixed with a little honey.

Lobster

Cooked lobster should smell sweet and look fresh. Lobster tails should be tightly curled. Lobster meat is so sweet and succulent that you don't want to miss a morsel. If you're not sure how to deal with a cooked lobster, study these steps so that you'll look like an expert. Grasp the head and body with two hands and twist them firmly in opposite directions, to release the tail. With scissors, cut down both sides of the shell on the underside, placing the scissors between the flesh and soft shell. Peel back the soft undershell to reveal the flesh. Gently pull out the flesh in one piece. Scrape the meat out of the claws with a lobster pick. Gently pull out the vein, starting at the head end.

This is a delicate dressing for lobster that won't overwhelm the flesh. Heat a tablespoon of oil in a pan, add a tablespoon of honey and 125 ml ($^1/_2$ cup) balsamic vinegar and bring to the boil, then boil until reduced by half.

Prawns

While cooked prawns are readily available, they are very easy to cook yourself and taste much better. Peel and devein (but keep the tails intact because they look prettier), then either grill (broil), steam, fry or boil for a few minutes until they become pink.

Here is a great Thai coriander sauce that's perfect for cooked prawns. Mix together 3 tablespoons sweet chilli sauce, 2 teaspoons lime juice and 1 tablespoon chopped coriander (cilantro) in a jug or bowl and drizzle over the cooked prawns.

chilli crab

2 x 250 g (9 oz) live crabs
2 tbs oil
1/2 tsp chilli sauce
1 tbs soy sauce
1 1/2 tsp rice vinegar
2 tbs Shaoxing rice wine
1/2 tsp salt
1 tbs sugar
1 tbs chicken stock
1/2 tsp grated fresh ginger
1 garlic clove, crushed
1 spring onion (scallion), finely chopped

To kill the crabs humanely, freeze them for an hour. Now plunge them into a large pot of boiling water for about a minute, then rinse them in cold water. Twist off and discard the upper shell, and discard the spongy grey gill tissue from inside the crab. Rinse the bodies and drain well. Cut away the last two hairy joints of the legs. Cut each crab into four to six pieces, cutting so that a portion of the body is attached to one or two legs. Crack the claws using crab crackers or the back of a cleaver.

Heat a wok over high heat, add a little of the oil and heat until very hot. Add half the crab and fry for several minutes to cook the meat right through. Remove and drain. Repeat with more oil and the rest of the crab.

Combine the chilli sauce, soy sauce, rice vinegar, rice wine, salt, sugar and stock.

Reheat the wok over high heat, add the remaining oil and heat until very hot. Stir-fry the ginger, garlic and spring onion for about 10 seconds. Add the sauce mixture to the wok and cook briefly. Add the crab pieces and toss lightly to coat with the moreish sauce. Put the wok lid on and cook for 5 minutes, then serve. Serves 2.

Licking your fingers clean of the spicy, salty zing is a must so that you don't miss out on any of the flavour.

Besides tasting fabulous, this dish features a vibrantly coloured mix of ingredients that make it an eye-catching addition to any table.

lamb cutlets with beetroot, bean and potato salad

1 garlic clove, crushed
1 tbs finely chopped thyme
3 tsp lemon juice
2 tsp walnut oil
1 tbs extra virgin olive oil
6 lamb cutlets, trimmed
3 baby beetroots, trimmed
250 g (9 oz) kipfler potatoes, unpeeled
125 g (4^1/$_2$ oz) baby green beans
1–2 tbs olive oil

For the dressing:
1 garlic clove, crushed
2 tbs lemon juice
2 tbs extra virgin olive oil
2 tsp walnut oil
2 tbs chopped walnuts

First, make a marinade out of the garlic, thyme, lemon juice, walnut oil and extra virgin olive oil. Add the lamb cutlets and smear them in the marinade. Cover with plastic wrap and pop in the fridge for the night.

Cook the beetroots and potatoes in boiling water, scooping the potatoes out with a slotted spoon after 12 minutes (they should be tender by then), and cooking the beetroots for another 8 minutes before draining. When both are cool enough to handle, peel them. Now cut each beetroot into six wedges and thickly slice the potatoes.

Cook the beans in lightly salted boiling water for 4 minutes. Drain, refresh under cold water, then drain again. Pat dry with paper towels.

Heat the oil in a large frying pan over high heat and cook the cutlets for a couple of minutes on each side, or until they are cooked how you like them.

Whisk the garlic, lemon juice and oils in a bowl. Add the potatoes, beans and walnuts and toss gently. Season and arrange over the beetroot. Top with the cutlets and serve. Serves 2.

beef fillet with onion marmalade

125 ml (1/2 cup) port
1 1/2 tbs balsamic vinegar
1 garlic clove, crushed
2 beef eye fillet steaks
1 tbs olive oil

For the onion marmalade:
1 1/2 tbs olive oil
250 g (9 oz) onions, thinly sliced
2 tbs soft brown sugar
2 tbs red wine vinegar

Make a marinade out of the port, vinegar and garlic — the best way is to put it in a large non-metallic dish that will fit the beef. Now add the beef and smear it in the marinade. Cover and pop in the fridge for at least 2 hours to absorb some of the flavour. Drain, reserving the marinade.

To make the marmalade, heat the oil in a large non-stick frying pan, add the onion and sugar and cook over medium heat until caramelized — be aware that this may take up to half an hour. Stir in the red wine vinegar, bring to the boil and cook until thick and sticky, 10 minutes or so. Remove from the heat and keep warm.

Heat the oil in a large frying pan, add the steaks and cook over high heat for 3–5 minutes on each side, or until cooked to how you like them. Remove from the pan and keep warm, then add the reserved marinade to the pan and boil until reduced by half.

Drizzle some of the sauce onto two serving plates, sit a steak on the sauce, top with a generous mound of onion marmalade and some steamed greens or creamy mash. Serves 2.

For full-blooded meat lovers who expect the best old-fashioned flavours — but with a decidedly modern edge.

When you're cooking with wine, it's worth using a decent one, if only because it's so nice to pour yourself a glass while you're preparing the meal — one for you, one for the beef...

beef with rich red wine sauce

2 tbs virgin olive oil
2 garlic cloves, crushed
400 g (14 oz) beef eye fillet
300 g (10½ oz) can cannellini beans, rinsed and drained
375 ml (1½ cups) beef stock
170 ml (⅔ cup) red wine
2 tbs tomato paste (purée)
1 tbs soft brown sugar

Make a simple marinade out of the oil and one of the crushed garlic cloves, then marinate the beef for 30 minutes.

Blitz the beans and remaining garlic in a food processor or blender until nice and smooth. With the motor running, add 1½ tablespoons of the stock and whizz until smooth. Season.

Heat a large deep frying pan over medium heat, add the beef and, brushing with the marinade, cook for 5 minutes, or until browned all over. Lift it into a roasting tin and roast for 15–20 minutes in a 200°C (400°F/Gas 6) oven, or until cooked to your liking. Cover and let it rest for 15 minutes.

While the meat is roasting, add the wine to the frying pan and stir, scraping the bottom to remove any yummy bits. Add the tomato paste, sugar and rest of the stock to the pan, then reduce the heat and simmer until the sauce has reduced by half, about 30 minutes. Gently heat the bean purée, then dollop it onto two plates. Arrange slices of the beef over the top and drizzle on the red wine sauce. Great served with steamed greens. Serves 2.

lamb cutlets with creamy spinach

4 frenched lamb cutlets
1 tbs olive oil
15 g (1/2 oz) butter
1 garlic clove, crushed
2 spring onions (scallions), sliced
200 g (7 oz) baby English spinach leaves, roughly chopped
2 tsp shredded basil
1 1/2 tbs cream
1 tbs wholegrain mustard
2 tomatoes, cut in half and roasted

Trim the lamb cutlets of any excess fat or sinew and lightly coat each cutlet in a little freshly ground black pepper.

Heat the oil in a frying pan and cook the cutlets over high heat for 3 minutes on each side, or until cooked to how you like them. Take them out of the pan and keep warm.

Melt the butter in the frying pan and add the garlic, spring onions and spinach. Cook until the spring onion is soft and the spinach wilts, then add the basil, cream and mustard. Cook until heated through and you have a lovely creamy, soft mass.

Make a bed of creamy spinach on two plates, then sit the lamb cutlets over the top. Serve with warmed roasted tomatoes on the side. Serves 2.

Like mashed potato, creamy spinach is a comforting treat for those times when you're in need of a little tenderness.

Once you've found a butcher that you like, it's worth nurturing the relationship, particularly if they stock good veal for special occasions.

veal scaloppine with white wine sauce

2 x 175 g (6 oz) veal escalopes
15 g (¹/₂ oz) butter
1–2 tbs dry white wine or dry marsala
(not sweet)
2–3 tbs thick (double/heavy) cream
2 tsp wholegrain mustard
1 tbs chopped flat-leaf (Italian) parsley

Lay the escalopes between two sheets of plastic wrap and smack them with the heel of your hand to flatten them a bit. Otherwise you can use a rolling pin, but don't be too violent or you'll tear the meat.

Fry the escalopes in the butter — depending how large your escalopes are, you may need to cook each one separately — for 1 minute on each side, or until just cooked. Take them out of the pan and keep them warm.

Splash in the wine, bring to the boil and cook until reduced by half, then stir in the cream, bring to a simmer and reduce by half again. Add the mustard and 2 teaspoons of the parsley and stir until you have a mustardy creamy sauce. Return the veal to the pan to warm through and coat in the sauce. Serve the veal with a little sauce and sprinkle with the remaining parsley. Great with boiled baby potatoes and a crisp green salad.
Serves 2.

succulent chargrilled lobster tails

70 g ($2\frac{1}{2}$ oz) butter
$1\frac{1}{2}$ tbs lemon juice
1 tbs chopped flat-leaf (Italian) parsley
1 small garlic clove, crushed
4 lobster tails in the shell
1 lemon, cut into wedges

Heat the butter in a small saucepan over medium heat until it begins to brown, about 3 minutes, but watch it carefully to make sure that it doesn't burn. Lower the heat and keep cooking until it is dark golden brown. Take the pan off the hob, stir in the lemon juice, parsley and garlic and season with salt and black pepper.

Cut the lobster tails lengthways and remove any digestive tract, but leave the meat in the shell. Brush the exposed lobster meat with lots of the lemony butter. Cook the lobster tails, cut-side down, on a chargrill pan (griddle) for 6 minutes, then turn them over and cook until the shells turn bright red, about 4 minutes.

While the lobster is cooking, cook the lemon wedges in the pan until they are marked and heated through — this will only take a minute or so. Arrange the lobster on serving plates and serve it with the chargrilled lemon wedges and the rest of the lemony butter as a dipping sauce. This is great with a green salad and some crusty bread to soak up the delicious juices.
Serves 2.

Going out to a restaurant and ordering lobster used to be the high point of a great dining experience. Now try the sheer decadence of eating it in your own home.

Fruit combines beautifully with all kinds of game meat, and duck is no exception. These breasts are rich and tasty without being overly fatty.

duck breasts with cassis and raspberries

2 x 200 g (7 oz) duck breasts
1 tsp sea salt
1 tsp ground cinnamon
2 tsp demerara sugar
125 ml (1/2 cup) red wine
4 tbs crème de cassis
2 tsp cornflour (cornstarch) or arrowroot
125 g (half a punnet) raspberries

Score the duck breasts through the skin and fat but not all the way through to the meat. Fry the duck breasts, skin-side down, until the skin browns and the fat runs out. Lift them out of the pan and tip away most of the fat.

Mix together the sea salt, cinnamon and sugar and smear it over the duck. Season with pepper. Reheat the frying pan and cook the duck breasts, skin-side up, for 10–15 minutes. Lift out of the frying pan and leave to rest.

Meanwhile, mix together the wine and cassis in a jug. Pour 2–3 tablespoons of the liquid into a small bowl and mix in the cornflour or arrowroot, then pour this back into the jug.

Pour the excess fat out of the frying pan to leave about 1 tablespoon. Return the pan to the heat and pour in the wine and cassis. Simmer, stirring constantly, until the sauce has thickened. Add the berries and simmer for another minute, to warm the fruit through.

To make the skin gorgeously crisp and tasty, briefly grill (broil) the duck, skin-side up. Slice the duck breasts thinly, pour a little sauce over the top and serve the rest in a jug. Serves 2.

This fancy version of strawberries and cream is easy to prepare and is great to share.

strawberries romanoff

250 g (1 punnet) strawberries, 2 whole strawberries set aside, the rest chopped
1¹/₂ tbs caster (superfine) sugar
2 tbs liqueur such as Cointreau or kirsch
150 ml (5 fl oz) thickened cream

Put the chopped strawberries in a bowl with the caster sugar and liqueur. Cover and refrigerate overnight so the strawberries become drunken treasures.

Beat the cream and stir in half the strawberries. Put the rest of the strawberries in the base of two whisky tumblers, divide the strawberry and cream mixture between the tumblers and decorate with a pretty whole strawberry.
Serves 2.

A dessert for the true romantic, the heart shape says it all.

coeur à la crème

85 g (3 oz) cottage cheese, drained
1 tbs icing (confectioners') sugar
100 ml (3 1/2 fl oz) cream, whipped
fresh berries

Blitz the cottage cheese in a food processor until you have a smooth, creamy mixture. Stir in the icing sugar, then fold in the cream to lighten the texture.

Line two coeur à la crème moulds (these are special heart-shaped moulds with drainage holes in the bottom) with muslin and fill with your creamy mass. Cover and leave to drain off overnight. Unmould your hearts and serve with fresh berries.
Serves 2.

caramelized figs with amaretto mascarpone

3 tbs caster (superfine) sugar
2 tbs cream
$1/2$ tsp vanilla essence
4 tbs mascarpone
2 tbs amaretto
1 tbs caster (superfine) sugar, extra
2 tbs blanched almonds, finely chopped
$1/4$ tsp ground cinnamon
4 fresh figs, halved

Make a syrup out of the caster sugar and 3 tablespoons water by stirring over low heat until the sugar dissolves. If any crystals appear, brush down the side of the pan with a clean brush dipped in water. Bring to the boil and cook, swirling occasionally (but not stirring), until the mixture is golden, about 8 minutes. Then quickly take the pan off the hob and pour in the cream and vanilla, stirring constantly until you have a smooth sauce.

To make the amaretto mascarpone, mix together the mascarpone, amaretto and 2 teaspoons of the extra caster sugar.

Combine the chopped almonds, cinnamon and remaining caster sugar on a plate.

Press the cut side of each fig half into the almond mixture, then place, cut-side up, onto a foil-lined baking tray. Cook under a hot grill (broiler) until the sugar has caramelized and the almonds are nicely toasted — watch carefully so they don't burn.

Arrange four fig halves on each plate, dollop some amaretto mascarpone to the side and drizzle with the sauce.
Serves 2.

Soft, hot, melting figs
drizzled with cool, creamy
mascarpone ... pure bliss.

With a flower in the centre of each jelly, these desserts look as beautiful as they taste. And who can resist a lovely dose of bubbly?

champagne and blueberry jellies

200 ml (7 fl oz) champagne
1 1/2 tsp gelatine
2 tbs caster (superfine) sugar
2 pansies or violets
25 g (1 oz) small blueberries

Pour the champagne into a saucepan with the gelatine and sugar and stir over low heat until the gelatine dissolves. Simmer for a couple of minutes, then take the pan off the hob and leave to cool slightly.

Lightly grease two 125 ml (1/2 cup) dariole moulds, and carefully place a pansy or violet in the centre of each base — position them so the flowers are face-side down. Pour enough of the champagne liquid over the flowers to just cover them. Refrigerate them until they set, keeping the rest of the liquid at room temperature so that it doesn't set.

Divide the berries between the moulds and pour over the remaining champagne liquid. Again, refrigerate until set.

To serve, use your fingers to release the jellies from their moulds. If you have trouble getting them out, rub the outsides of the moulds with a warm cloth to slightly melt the jelly and they should slip out easily.
Serves 2.

chocolate truffles

300 g (10½ oz) good-quality dark chocolate, finely chopped (the quality of the chocolate will really make or break this recipe, so do use the best you can find)
100 ml (3½ fl oz) thick (double) cream
1 tsp vanilla essence
good-quality cocoa powder (again, use good stuff)

The first step is to make ganache. Put the chopped chocolate in a bowl. Put the cream and vanilla in a small saucepan and heat until it is just at boiling point. Now pour the hot cream onto the chopped chocolate. Gently mix with a whisk until the mixture is glossy and smooth. If there are any lumps, you'll need to sit the bowl over a pan of barely steaming water, off the heat, and lightly stir for a moment to melt any remaining chocolate — the trick here is not to overheat the chocolate mass. Refrigerate until it is set.

Form the ganache into small balls — you can either be precise and use a melon baller or be a bit looser and form rough balls with your hands. Once you have your balls, pop them back into the fridge to set. When set, it's time to roll them in cocoa. However, if you've done neat balls, perfect them by first rolling them between your palms, then in the cocoa.

They now need an hour in a cool place to set, but if you've been very organized and made these ahead of time, you can keep them in the fridge. They will probably need another light dusting of cocoa powder before you serve them.
Makes about 25.

Just one or two handmade truffles add the finishing touch to a memorable meal. Use only the very best dark chocolate you can find.

From gelato to panna cotta to tiramisu, it seems the Italians have mastered the art of making classic cold desserts. This zabaglione is no exception.

frozen zabaglione with marsala sauce

2 egg yolks
1/2 tsp vanilla essence
4 tbs sweet Marsala
2 tbs caster (superfine) sugar
4 tbs cream, whipped to firm peaks
2 tbs whole blanched almonds,
toasted and chopped

Put the egg yolks, vanilla, most of the Marsala and half of the sugar in a non-metallic bowl and whisk well.

Sit the bowl on top of a saucepan one-third full of simmering water, making sure the base of the bowl does not touch the water. Whisk continuously for 5 minutes, or until foamy and thick enough that it holds its form when you drizzle some from the whisk.

Take the pan off the heat and sit in a bowl of ice, whisking until cool. Take out of the ice, then gently fold in the whipped cream and almonds. Carefully pour into two 125 ml (1/2 cup) dariole moulds or ramekins, cover with plastic wrap and freeze until firm — this is not a quick process; more like 6 hours.

Combine the remaining Marsala and sugar in a small saucepan and stir over low heat until the sugar dissolves. Bring just to the boil, then reduce the heat and simmer until just syrupy, 5 minutes or so. Take off the hob.

Briefly dip the moulds into warm water, then loosen with a knife. Turn out onto a plate and drizzle with syrup.
Serves 2.

zesty tropical fruit salad

500 g (1 lb 2 oz) watermelon,
cut into large pieces
half a small pineapple, peeled and
chopped
1 mango, sliced
half a guava, sliced
half a small red papaya, cut into
large pieces
6 lychees, peeled
1 kiwi fruit, sliced

For the syrup:
$1^{1}/_{2}$ tbs lime juice
4 tbs grated light palm sugar or
soft brown sugar
3 star anise seeds (the seeds are
inside the pods of the star)
1 vanilla bean, split in half
1 pandanus leaf, knotted
zest of half a lime

The first step is to combine all the carefully chopped and sliced up fruit in a bowl — you'll be serving the fruit salad in this bowl, so choose an attractive one.

Now for the syrup. Put the lime juice, palm sugar, star anise, vanilla bean, pandanus leaf, lime zest and 125 ml ($1/2$ cup) water in a saucepan and stir over low heat until the sugar dissolves. Once this happens, bring to the boil, reduce the heat and simmer until the syrup is reduced by half — 10 minutes at the most. Leave somewhere to cool slightly.

Pour your tropical syrup over the fruit and pop the whole lot in the fridge until cold. Serves 2.

If you are bored (and rightfully so) with the predictable mix of apples, bananas and oranges, try this tantalizing combination of exotic fruits.

The two key ingredients — watermelon and vodka — combine to make a deliciously refreshing adult's-only sort of slush. Serve them with style in shot glasses.

summery vodka granita

500 g (1 lb 2 oz) piece of watermelon, rind removed to give 300 g (10½ oz) flesh
1 tsp lime juice
1½ tbs caster (superfine) sugar
1½ tbs citrus-flavoured vodka

Roughly chop the watermelon to try to get rid of as many seeds as possible. Put the flesh in a food processor and add the lime juice and sugar. Process until smooth, then strain through a fine sieve. Stir in the vodka, then taste a little — depending on how sweet the watermelon is, you may have to add a little more sugar.

Pour into a shallow 750 ml (3 cup) metal tin and freeze until it's beginning to harden around the edges, about 30 minutes. Then scrape the frozen parts back into the mixture with a fork and pop back into the freezer. Repeat this pattern every 30 minutes for about 4 hours, or until even ice crystals have formed.

Serve immediately or beat with a fork just before serving. To serve, scrape into dishes with a fork.
Serves 2.

gooey camembert with port-soaked raisins

2 tbs raisins
2 tbs port
375 g (13 oz) whole round
Camembert cheese
oil spray
almond biscotti

For plump, moist, port-soaked raisins, combine the raisins and port in a small saucepan. Bring to the boil briefly, then cool for half an hour.

Cut a neat circular lid from the top of the Camembert, leaving a 2 cm (3/4 inch) border. Carefully remove the lid and scoop out the soft cheese with a teaspoon, leaving the base intact. Put the raisins in the hole and top with the cheese, squashing it down so that as much as possible fits back into the cavity, then replace the lid.

Spray a double layer of foil with oil and wrap it around the Camembert to form a sealed parcel. Cook the parcel in a 200°C (400°F/ Gas 6) oven for 15–20 minutes, by which stage the cheese should be soft, gooey and warmed right through. Use almond biscotti as a sort of edible scoop.
Serves 2–4.

Melted Camembert is pure indulgence, so prepare yourself for an oozy, sticky, smelly treat — perfect at the end of the evening with a glass of port.

spicy
food that bites back

A Bloody Mary is refreshing, invigorating and just the thing to serve at a recovery brunch.

bloody mary

3 ice cubes
45 ml (1½ fl oz) vodka
4 drops of Tabasco sauce
1 tsp Worcestershire sauce
10 ml (¼ fl oz) lemon juice
60 ml (2 fl oz) chilled tomato juice
1 celery stalk

Put the ice cubes in a highball glass, pour in the vodka, then add the Tabasco, Worcestershire sauce and lemon juice. Add a pinch of salt and a grind of black pepper, then pour in the tomato juice and stir well. Allow to sit for a minute and then garnish with the celery.
Serves 1.

Here's a sure-fire pick-me-up for those days when you need something non-alcoholic with a little bite.

virgin mary

lemon wedge
2 tsp celery salt
1 tsp black pepper
ice cubes
125 ml (4 fl oz) chilled tomato juice
15 ml (1/2 fl oz) lemon juice
1 tsp Worcestershire sauce
dash of Tabasco sauce
celery stalk

Run the lemon wedge around the rim of a large goblet, then dip the rim in a saucer that you've sprinkled with celery salt and pepper — you should end up with an encrusted rim.

Half-fill a cocktail shaker with ice. Pour in the tomato juice, lemon juice, Worcestershire sauce and Tabasco and shake well. Strain into the goblet, then garnish with the celery. Serves 1.

Although there are many ready-made curry pastes and marinades available, they will never come close to the flavour you achieve if you whip one up yourself.

chicken tikka

For the marinade:
2 tsp paprika
1 tsp chilli powder
2 tbs garam masala
1/4 tsp tandoori food colouring
(optional)
1 1/2 tbs lemon juice
4 garlic cloves, roughly chopped
5 cm (2 inch) piece of fresh ginger,
roughly chopped
3 tbs chopped coriander (cilantro) leaves
100 ml (3 1/2 fl oz) thick natural yoghurt

500 g (1 lb 2 oz) skinless chicken breast
fillets, cut into 2.5 cm (1 inch) cubes
wedges of lemon

The basis to a good Chicken tikka is the marinade. It's simple to make, but full of flavour — blitz all the ingredients together in a food processor until you have a smooth, creamy mixture. Another way to approach it is to chop the garlic, ginger and coriander leaves more finely and mix with the rest of the marinade ingredients. Taste a little of the marinade, then season with a little salt.

Put the chicken cubes in a bowl with the marinade and mix thoroughly. Cover and marinate overnight in the fridge so the chicken soaks up as much flavour as possible.

Thread the chicken pieces onto four metal skewers and put them on a metal rack above a baking tray. Roast in a 200°C (400°F/Gas 6) oven until the chicken is cooked through and browned around the edges, about 20 minutes. Serve with wedges of lemon to squeeze over the chicken for a bit of zing.
Serves 4 as a snack.

thai fish cakes with sweet chilli sauce

For the cucumber dipping sauce:
1 Lebanese (short) cucumber, seeded and finely diced
2 small red chillies, finely chopped
4 tbs grated palm sugar or soft brown sugar
6 tbs rice vinegar
1 tbs chopped coriander (cilantro) leaves

500 g (1 lb 2 oz) skinless redfish fillets
200 g (7 oz) raw prawns (shrimp), peeled and deveined
3 tbs Thai red curry paste
50 g (1³/4 oz) snake beans, sliced
4 makrut (kaffir) lime leaves, finely shredded
6 Thai or normal basil leaves, shredded
oil, for deep-frying

Start with the dipping sauce because once it's made you can leave it alone while you move on to the fish cakes. Combine the cucumber, chillies, sugar, rice vinegar, coriander and 1 tablespoon water in a bowl and mix well to dissolve the sugar.

Now for the fish cakes. Put the fish, prawns and curry paste in a food processor and whizz into a smooth, sticky paste. Scoop into a bowl and get your hands in there to mix in the beans, lime leaves and basil. Shape the mixture into small balls (about a tablespoon per ball works well), then flatten them with the palm of your hand. Cover and refrigerate for an hour.

Deep-fry the fish cakes in batches until browned and cooked through, about 2 minutes. Drain on paper towels and serve with the cucumber dipping sauce.
Serves 4–6 as a snack.

Known as *tod man pla* in Thailand, these little fish patties are eaten as spicy snacks with sweet chilli sauce.

Spareribs make licky, sticky finger food at a casual gathering of friends. Be sure to pass around plenty of paper napkins as things may get rather messy.

barbecued chilli pork ribs

1 kg (2 lb 4 oz) pork spareribs
125 g (4½ oz) canned puréed tomatoes
2 tbs honey
2 tbs chilli sauce
2 tbs hoisin sauce
2 tbs lime juice
2 garlic cloves, crushed
1 tbs oil

Cut each rib into thirds, then lay in a single layer in a shallow non-metallic dish.

Mix together all the other ingredients, except the oil, and pour over the meat. Now swoosh everything around to make sure every piece of the meat is coated in the marinade. Cover with plastic wrap and refrigerate overnight, turning every now and then.

Preheat a barbecue grill or chargrill pan (griddle) and brush it lightly with oil. Drain the ribs, reserving the marinade, and cook them over medium heat, basting with the marinade and turning over occasionally until tender and well browned, about 15 minutes. Season, then serve hot with a green salad and a pile of serviettes (napkins) for sticky fingers. Serves 4–6 as a snack.

gyoza

150 g (5 1/2 oz) Chinese cabbage, very finely shredded
225 g (8 oz) minced (ground) pork
2 garlic cloves, finely chopped
2 tsp finely chopped fresh ginger
2 spring onions (scallions), finely chopped
2 tsp cornflour (cornstarch)
1 tbs light soy sauce
2 tsp Chinese rice wine
2 tsp sesame oil
40 round Shanghai dumpling wrappers (made out of flour and water)
2 tbs vegetable oil
125 ml (1/2 cup) chicken stock
soy sauce or Chinese black vinegar

Put the cabbage in a colander and then salt it with 1/2 teaspoon salt. Leave for 30 minutes to drain, stirring every now and then.

Put the minced (ground) pork, garlic, ginger, spring onions, cornflour, soy sauce, rice wine and sesame oil in a bowl and mix it all together — preferably with your hands.

Rinse the cabbage under cold water. Dry with paper towels, then mix into the pork mixture.

Get your wrappers ready. Fill each one with about a teaspoon of the pork mixture, then brush the edge with a little water. Now fold in half to form a semicircle. Using your thumb and index finger, create a pleat, pressing firmly as you do and gently tapping the gyoza on a work surface to form a flat bottom.

Cook the gyoza in batches (you'll probably have at least four batches) for 2 minutes, flat-side down. Once they are all cooked, return them to the pan (again in batches), this time adding some stock and shaking the pan to unstick the gyoza. Cover and cook until the liquid has evaporated, about 4 minutes. Serve with soy sauce or Chinese black vinegar. Serves 6–8 as a snack.

A traditional Chinese dumpling that has become increasingly popular in Japan, gyoza can also be made with chicken or beef mince, or even seafood.

For a feisty, fiery hit, marinate the chicken overnight so the flesh absorbs as much flavour as possible.

spiced portuguese chicken

1 small red onion, chopped
4 garlic cloves, chopped
2 tsp grated lemon zest
1$\frac{1}{2}$ tsp chilli flakes
1 tsp smoked paprika
2 tbs oil
2 tbs red wine vinegar
1.5 kg (3 lb 5 oz) whole chicken
4 tbs chopped parsley
lemon wedges, to serve

Put the onion, garlic, lemon zest, chilli flakes, paprika, oil and vinegar in a food processor and blitz into a smooth paste.

The idea with the chicken is to cut it open and flatten it out — poultry shears are the easiest for this. Cut the chicken down the backbone and press down on the breastbone until it's flattened. Now score the flesh with a sharp knife (so the spicy flavours of the marinade get a chance to be absorbed) and smear the spice mixture all over the chicken. Cover and refrigerate overnight.

Lay the flattened chicken, skin-side up, under a hot grill (broiler) and cook until lightly browned, about 10 minutes. Transfer to a roasting tin and roast for 35–40 minutes in a 200°C (400°F/Gas 6) oven, by which time it should be cooked through.

Sprinkle the chicken with the parsley and drizzle with any pan juices. Serve with lemon wedges and a green salad.
Serves 4.

chicken and noodle soup

1 litre (4 cups) chicken stock
1 star anise
4 very thin slices of fresh ginger
400 g (14 oz) chicken breast fillets
375 g (13 oz) Shanghai noodles
1 tbs Chinese rice wine
1 tbs julienned fresh ginger
1^1/$_2$ tbs light soy sauce
^{1}/$_2$ tsp sugar
150 g (5^1/$_2$ oz) fresh asparagus,
cut into 3 cm (1^1/$_4$ inch) lengths
4 spring onions (scallions) (white and some
green parts), thinly sliced on diagonal
50 g (1^3/$_4$ oz) watercress, tips
picked off the stems
^{1}/$_4$ tsp sesame oil
light soy sauce, extra, to serve

Pour the stock and 500 ml (2 cups) water into a large saucepan and bring to the boil. Reduce to a simmer, then throw in the star anise, ginger slices and chicken and simmer until the chicken is cooked through, about 15 minutes. Lift the chicken out of the stock with a slotted spoon and set aside somewhere to cool. Discard the star anise and ginger, but keep the stock in the pan.

Meanwhile, bring 2 litres (8 cups) water to the boil in a large saucepan and cook the noodles for about 5 minutes. Drain, then rinse under cold water to refresh the noodles.

Thinly slice the chicken. Return the stock to the boil, then add the rice wine, julienned ginger, soy sauce, sugar, asparagus and ^{1}/$_2$ teaspoon salt, stir well. Reduce the heat, add the noodles and simmer for 2 minutes. Return the chicken to the pan to heat through.

Gently remove the noodles from the soup with tongs and evenly divide among six bowls. Spoon the chicken, asparagus, spring onions and watercress into the bowls, then ladle on the stock. Drizzle with sesame oil and serve with extra soy sauce, if desired. Serves 6.

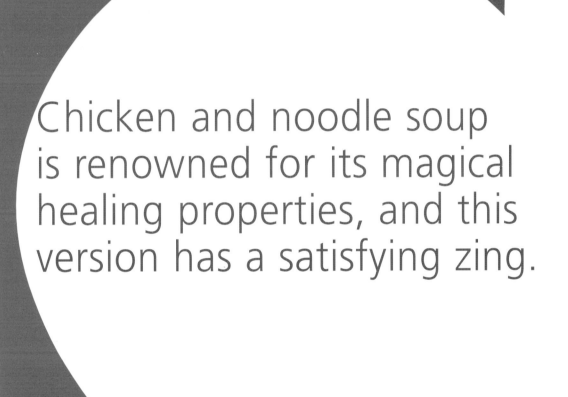

Chicken and noodle soup is renowned for its magical healing properties, and this version has a satisfying zing.

A favourite with children and even those adults who like to pretend they've outgrown peanut butter. It's unusual to find yourself with any leftover satays.

beef satay

2 small garlic cloves, crushed
3 tsp grated fresh ginger
1 tbs fish sauce
700 g (1 lb 9 oz) rump steak, cut into 2.5 cm (1 inch) cubes
2 small red chillies, seeded and julienned

For the satay sauce:
8 red Asian shallots, finely chopped
8 garlic cloves, crushed
4 small red chillies, finely chopped
1 tbs finely chopped fresh ginger
1 tbs peanut oil
250 g (1 cup) crunchy peanut butter
400 ml (14 fl oz) coconut milk
1 tbs soy sauce
4 tbs grated palm sugar or soft brown sugar
3 tbs fish sauce
1 kaffir lime leaf
4 tbs lime juice

First of all, make the marinade for the beef. Combine the garlic, ginger and fish sauce and smear it all over the beef. Now marinate, covered, in the fridge for at least 3 hours, or longer if you can spare the time. At the same time, soak eight wooden skewers in cold water for an hour so that you don't end up with a blazing inferno (of course, if you're using metal skewers, you can skip this step).

To make the satay sauce, cook the shallots, garlic, chillies and ginger in the oil until the shallots are golden, stirring often. Reduce the heat to low and add the peanut butter, coconut milk, soy sauce, palm sugar, fish sauce, lime leaf and lime juice. Simmer until you have a thick, rich peanuty sauce — 10 minutes should do it. Now fish out the lime leaf.

Thread the beef onto the skewers and cook on a chargrill pan (griddle) over high heat until cooked though, turning halfway. Dollop on some satay sauce and garnish with the julienned chillies. Serve with mounds of steamed rice.
Serves 4.

chicken laksa

2–3 tsp shrimp paste
1 1/2 tbs ground coriander
1 tbs ground cumin
1 tsp ground turmeric
1 onion, roughly chopped
1 tbs roughly chopped fresh ginger
3 garlic cloves, peeled
3 stems lemon grass (white part only), sliced
6 candlenuts or macadamias
4–6 small red chillies
1 litre (4 cups) chicken stock
3 tbs oil
400 g (14 oz) chicken thigh fillets, cut into 2 cm (3/4 inch) pieces
750 ml (3 cups) coconut milk
4 makrut (kaffir) lime leaves
2 1/2 tbs lime juice
2 tbs fish sauce
2 tbs grated palm sugar or soft brown sugar
250 g (9 oz) dried rice vermicelli
90 g (3 1/4 oz) bean sprouts
4 fried tofu puffs, julienned
3 tbs roughly chopped Vietnamese mint
20 g (2/3 cup) coriander (cilantro) leaves
lime wedges

The shrimp paste needs to be roasted — wrap it in foil and pop under a hot grill (broiler) for a minute. Scoop it into a food processor or blender with all the spices, onion, ginger, garlic, lemon grass, candlenuts, chillies and 125 ml (1/2 cup) of the stock and blitz into a paste.

Heat the oil in a wok or large saucepan over low heat and gently cook the paste for about 4 minutes, stirring constantly so that it doesn't burn or stick to the bottom. Pour in the remaining stock and bring to the boil over high heat. Reduce the heat to medium and simmer away until it thickens slightly, say for 15 minutes. Add the chicken and simmer until cooked through, about 4–5 minutes.

Add the coconut milk, lime leaves, lime juice, fish sauce and palm sugar and simmer for another 5 minutes, without letting it boil.

Meanwhile, put the vermicelli in a heatproof bowl, cover with boiling water and soak until soft and pliant, about 6 minutes. Drain and divide the vermicelli and bean sprouts among large serving bowls. Ladle the hot soup over the top and garnish with some tofu strips, mint and coriander. Serve with a lime wedge. Serves 4–6.

If you find the sheer number of ingredients involved in Thai cooking too intimidating for just one meal, then double or triple the quantities of the laksa paste and store in a jar in the fridge for a quick spice hit another time.

Dried chillies impart a smooth, smoky flavour that can't be gained by using fresh ones.

penne arrabbiata

2 tbs olive oil
2 large garlic cloves, thinly sliced
1–2 dried chillies
800 g (1 lb 12 oz) canned tomatoes
400 g (14 oz) penne rigate or rigatoni
1 basil sprig, torn into pieces

Heat the olive oil in a saucepan and add the garlic and chillies. Gently cook the garlic until it becomes light golden brown. Turn the chillies over during cooking so both sides get a chance to infuse the oil with their slightly nutty flavour. Add the tomatoes and season with salt. Cook gently, breaking up the tomatoes with a wooden spoon, for about half an hour, or until the sauce is rich and thick. If you like a lot of heat in your food, break the chillies open to release the seeds, otherwise fish them out.

Meanwhile, cook the pasta in a pot of boiling salted water until *al dente*. Drain.

Just before serving, add the basil and some salt and pepper to the sauce, then toss with the pasta.
Serves 4.

chilli linguine with scallops and lime

40 g (1¹/₂ oz) butter
6 spring onions (scallions), sliced
1 tsp grated fresh ginger
2 garlic cloves, crushed
1 red chilli, finely chopped
500 g (1 lb 2 oz) scallops
zest and juice of 1 lime
400 ml (14 fl oz) coconut cream
2 tbs fish sauce
1 tbs soft brown sugar
6 makrut (kaffir) lime leaves,
finely shredded,
plus a little extra for garnish
250 g (9 oz) fresh chilli linguine (if you
have trouble finding this, use normal
fresh linguine and add an extra chilli
to the sauce)

Melt most of the butter in a large frying pan, then cook the spring onions, ginger, garlic and chilli for a couple of minutes until the spring onions wilt and become lightly golden. Remove from the pan.

Reheat the pan to high, add the remaining butter and cook the scallops in batches over high heat until tender — they won't need long at all. Scoop the spring onion mixture back into the pan and then stir in the lime zest and juice, coconut cream, fish sauce, brown sugar and lime leaves. Simmer just long enough for the sauce to heat through, about 5 minutes.

Meanwhile, cook the pasta in a large saucepan of boiling water until *al dente*, then drain well and twist into natty little nests. Dollop the sauce over the pasta and garnish with a few shredded lime leaves for a burst of colour.
Serves 4.

The Italians consider it a definite no-no to sprinkle Parmesan cheese on seafood … but if you want to buck tradition, who's to stop you?

phad thai

250 g (9 oz) narrow, dried rice-stick noodles
3 red Asian shallots
3 garlic cloves, chopped
1 small red chilli, chopped
4 tbs peanut oil
12 raw prawns (shrimp), peeled and deveined, with the tails intact
100 g (3¹/₂ oz) firm tofu, diced
2 tbs tamarind purée combined with 2 tbs water
2 eggs, lightly beaten
2 tbs fish sauce
2 tbs lime juice
2 tbs grated palm sugar or soft brown sugar
2 tbs dried shrimp
100 g (3¹/₂ oz) bean sprouts
30 g (1 cup) coriander (cilantro) sprigs
3 tbs roasted peanuts, roughly chopped
lime wedges, to serve

First of all, cover the noodles in boiling water and allow to soak for 15 minutes until they are soft and pliant. Drain well.

Pound the shallots, garlic and chilli in a mortar and pestle into a fine paste.

Heat 1 tablespoon of the oil in a wok, add the prawns and stir-fry until the prawns are pink and tender. Remove from the wok.

Heat the remaining oil in the wok, add the paste and stir-fry over medium heat until fragrant. Add the tofu and stir-fry until golden and slightly crisp. Now add the soaked noodles and the tamarind purée and toss until the noodles are evenly coated in the paste. Push the noodles to one side of the wok and pour in the beaten egg. Stir to break it up, then stir in the fish sauce, lime juice, palm sugar, dried shrimp, cooked prawns and half the bean sprouts. Serve in big bowls garnished with the remaining bean sprouts, coriander, peanuts and lime wedges. Serves 4.

It's no wonder that Thai cuisine has taken off so dramatically in recent years. With such a huge variety of flavours and spices, you could eat something different every night of the year.

Fortunately, there is a way to make good tandoori food without having to invest in a tandoor oven or move to India.

tandoori chicken

1.5 kg (3 lb 5 oz) skinless chicken
thighs and drumsticks
2 tbs ghee
lemon wedges

For the marinade:
2 tsp coriander seeds
1 tsp cumin seeds
1 onion, roughly chopped
3 garlic cloves, roughly chopped
5 cm (2 inch) piece of fresh ginger,
roughly chopped
250 ml (1 cup) thick natural yoghurt
grated zest of 1 lemon
3 tbs lemon juice
2 tbs vinegar
1 tsp paprika
2 tsp garam masala
1/2 tsp tandoori food colouring (optional)

Start with the chicken — trim away any excess fat and make an incision in each piece.

Move on to the marinade. Dry-fry first the coriander seeds, then the cumin seeds until aromatic. Now grind or crush them to a fine powder. Scoop into a food processor and add the rest of the the marinade ingredients, then whizz into a smooth paste. Season with salt.

Marinate the chicken in the marinade for at least 8 hours, or overnight, turning occasionally.

Sit the chicken on a wire rack on a baking tray. Cover with foil and roast on the top shelf of a 200°C (400°F/Gas 6) oven for about 45–50 minutes, or until cooked through (test by inserting a skewer into a thigh — the juices should run clear). Baste the chicken with the marinade once during cooking. Remove the foil 15 minutes before the end of cooking, to brown the tandoori mixture.

While the chicken is still on the rack, heat the ghee, pour it over the chicken pieces and cook under a hot grill (broiler) for 5 minutes, to blacken the edges of the chicken like a tandoor. Serve garnished with lemon wedges. Serves 4.

mee grob

oil, for deep-frying
300 g (10$^{1}/_{2}$ oz) dried Chinese vermicelli
2 eggs, lightly beaten
4 garlic cloves, finely chopped
150 g (5$^{1}/_{2}$ oz) minced (ground)
raw prawn (shrimp) meat
125 g (4$^{1}/_{2}$ oz) minced (ground) pork
200 g (7 oz) firm tofu, diced
90 g ($^{1}/_{2}$ cup) grated light palm sugar or
soft brown sugar
2 tbs fish sauce
4 tbs lime juice
2 tbs coconut vinegar
100 g (3$^{1}/_{2}$ oz) bean sprouts
2 tbs chopped coriander (cilantro) leaves
sliced small red chillies

Heat the oil in a wok until hot, or until a few vermicelli bubble on the surface of the oil when added. Cook the vermicelli in batches until puffed, crisp and golden. Drain away some of the oil on crumpled paper towels.

Remove all but 2 tablespoons of oil from the wok. Add the beaten egg and allow it to set into a sort of egg pancake, then turn and cook the other side. Remove and cut into thin slices — one easy way is to roll the pancake as if it were a carpet, then slice through the roll.

Add a little more oil to the wok, if necessary, then briefly cook the garlic, stirring so that it doesn't burn. Stir-fry the prawn, pork and tofu until just cooked. Now stir in the sugar, fish sauce, lime juice and vinegar and let it boil until it becomes thick and syrupy, about 3 minutes. Take the wok off the hob and stir in the vermicelli, bean sprouts and coriander. Serve immediately in bowls, topped with shredded egg and sliced chillies.
Serves 4.

For fresh, fast food, you can't go past Chinese or Thai. Once you've prepared the ingredients, it's just a matter of a few minutes of wok cooking, then you've got the rest of the night to relax.

This fiery feast is for those who like their flavours burning hot. Serve with plenty of yoghurt or raita to cool things down a bit.

pork vindaloo

1 kg (2 lb 4 oz) leg of pork on the bone
6 cardamom pods
1 tsp black peppercorns
4 dried chillies
1 tsp cloves
10 cm (4 inch) piece of cinnamon stick,
roughly broken
1 tsp cumin seeds
1/2 tsp ground turmeric
1/2 tsp coriander seeds
1/4 tsp fenugreek seeds
4 tbs vinegar
1 tbs balsamic vinegar
4 tbs oil
2 onions, thinly sliced
10 garlic cloves, thinly sliced
5 cm (2 inch) piece of fresh ginger,
cut into matchsticks
3 ripe tomatoes, roughly chopped
4 green chillies, chopped
1 tsp soft brown sugar

Trim away any excess fat from the pork, remove the bone and cut the pork into 2.5 cm (1 inch) cubes. Reserve the bone.

Split open the cardamom pods and remove the seeds. Finely grind the cardamom seeds, peppercorns, dried chillies, cloves, cinnamon stick, cumin seeds, turmeric, coriander seeds and fenugreek seeds in a spice grinder or mortar and pestle.

In a large bowl, mix the ground spices together with the vinegars. Add the pork and mix thoroughly to coat well. Cover and marinate in the fridge for 3 hours.

Heat the oil in a casserole dish over low heat and fry the onions until lightly browned. Add the garlic, ginger, tomatoes and chillies and stir well. Add the pork, increase the heat to high and fry until browned, about 4 minutes. Add 250 ml (1 cup) water and any of the marinade liquid left in the bowl, reduce the heat and bring slowly back to the boil. Add the sugar and the pork bone. Cover tightly and simmer for about 1 1/2 hours, stirring occasionally until the meat is very tender. Discard the bone. Season to taste with salt. Serves 4.

lamb korma

1 kg (2 lb 4 oz) boneless leg or shoulder
of lamb, cut into 2.5 cm (1 inch) cubes
2 tbs thick natural yoghurt
1 tbs coriander seeds
2 tsp cumin seeds
5 cardamom pods
2 onions
2 tbs grated coconut
1 tbs white poppy seeds (optional)
3 green chillies, roughly chopped
4 garlic cloves, crushed
5 cm (2 inch) piece of fresh ginger, grated
1 tbs cashew nuts
6 cloves
1/4 tsp ground cinnamon
2 tbs oil

Coat the lamb in the yoghurt and set aside. Dry-fry first the coriander seeds, then the cumin seeds over low heat until aromatic. Now grind or pound into a fine powder. Remove the seeds from the cardamom pods and grind them.

Roughly chop one onion and finely slice the other. Put just the chopped onion in a blender with the ground spices, coconut, poppy seeds, chillies, garlic, ginger, cashew nuts, cloves, cinnamon and 150 ml (5 fl oz) water and blitz into a smooth paste.

Heat the oil in a casserole dish over medium heat. Add the thinly sliced onion and fry until lightly browned. Pour the blended mixture into the casserole dish, season with salt and cook over low heat for 1 minute, or until the liquid evaporates and the sauce thickens. Add the lamb with the yoghurt and slowly bring to the boil. Cover tightly and simmer for 1 1/2 hours, or until the meat is very tender. Stir the meat occasionally to prevent it from sticking to the bottom of the dish. If the water has evaporated during the cooking time, add another 125 ml (1/2 cup) water to make a sauce. The sauce should be quite thick. Serves 4.

Lamb korma has the sort of wonderful, wafting aroma that makes people walking by your house drool. And it's the perfect introduction to spicy food — there is just a hint of spice in the mild creaminess of the sauce.

Fresh green chillies, galangal, lemon grass and spices are the base for the curry paste used in this popular Thai-style meal.

green chicken curry

For the curry paste:

1 tsp cumin seeds

1 tsp coriander seeds

1/4 tsp white peppercorns

2 stems lemon grass, white part only, chopped

10 long green chillies, trimmed

3 garlic cloves, roughly chopped

5 x 2 cm (2 x 3/4 inch) piece of fresh galangal or ginger, peeled and chopped

6 red Asian shallots, roughly chopped

5 coriander roots

2 tsp shrimp paste

1 tsp grated lime zest

1 tbs lime juice

1 tbs fish sauce

250 ml (1 cup) coconut cream

750 g (1 lb 10 oz) chicken thigh fillets, cut into thin strips about 1.5 cm (5/8 inch) thick

125 g (41/2 oz) snake beans, cut into 3 cm (11/4 inch) lengths

150 g (51/2 oz) broccoli, cut into small florets

100 g (31/2 oz) bamboo shoots, cut into thick strips

4 makrut (kaffir) lime leaves

500 ml (2 cups) coconut milk

1 tbs grated palm sugar or soft brown sugar

2–3 tbs fish sauce

30 g (1/2 cup) basil

The curry paste is the base of this recipe. To make it, dry-fry the cumin seeds, coriander seeds and peppercorns until fragrant, keeping the pan moving so they don't burn. Now grind them or crush them into a powder. Put in a food processor with the rest of the paste ingredients and 1/2 teaspoon ground black pepper and 1/4 teaspoon salt and blend to a smooth paste. Transfer to a ceramic or glass bowl, cover tightly (or the smell will taint everything in the fridge) and refrigerate.

Pour the coconut cream into a wok or heavy-based saucepan, bring to the boil and cook over high heat for 10 minutes, or until it 'cracks', which means the oil separates. This helps thicken the sauce. Reduce the heat to medium, stir in half the curry paste and cook for 2–3 minutes, or until fragrant.

Add the chicken and cook it through, which will take for a few minutes. Stir in the beans, broccoli, bamboo shoots, lime leaves and coconut milk. Bring to the boil, then reduce the heat and simmer until the beans are cooked but still firm to the bite. Stir in the sugar, fish sauce and basil. Serve with rice to soak up the juices.
Serves 4–6.

roast peppered beef

1 kg (2 lb 4 oz) piece of beef sirloin
2 tbs freshly ground black peppercorns
1 large red onion
4 large potatoes
50 g (1¾ oz) butter
3 tbs beef stock
3 tbs red wine
500 g (1 lb 2 oz) mixed yellow and
green beans

Take your piece of beef and trim most of the fat, leaving only a thin layer, so the meat will stay moist during cooking. Now stick the peppercorns over the beef — either press them on with your hands or roll the beef in them.

Cut the onion and potatoes into 5 mm (¼ inch) thick slices and put them in a roasting tin. Sit the beef on top, fatty side up. Cut most of the butter into small pieces and dot all over the beef and potatoes. Pour in the stock and wine and bake in a 180°C (350°F/Gas 4) oven for 35–40 minutes for medium–rare, or until cooked to your liking. Remove the beef from the oven and rest for at least 5 minutes before carving.

Meanwhile, bring a saucepan of lightly salted water to the boil. Add the mixed beans and cook until just tender, only about 3 minutes. Drain well, then add the remaining butter and toss together until they are shiny and slippery. Keep them warm until ready to serve.

To serve, divide the onion and potato mixture among four serving plates and top with slices of beef. Slosh on any yummy pan juices and serve with the beans.
Serves 4.

This peppery beef is ideal served as a warming winter meal, but when cooked in a kettle barbecue it makes for surprisingly good summer fare.

steamy
something hot, hot, hot

cinnamon porridge with figs and cream

200 g (2 cups) rolled oats
1/4 tsp ground cinnamon
50 g (1 3/4 oz) butter
95 g (1/2 cup) brown sugar
300 ml (10 fl oz) cream
6 fresh figs, halved
milk
thick (double/heavy) cream

The first step is to make the porridge. Put the oats, cinnamon and 1 litre (4 cups) water in a saucepan and stir until you have a thick, hot, smooth porridge, about 5 minutes. Take the pan off the hob while you prepare the rest of the meal.

Melt the butter in a large frying pan and when it's sizzling, add all but 2 tablespoons of the brown sugar and give a good stir until it dissolves into a gorgeous caramel butter. Pour the cream into the pan and bring to the boil. Now let the caramely cream simmer until it starts to thicken slightly, 2 minutes or so.

Lay the figs on a baking tray, sprinkle with the remaining sugar and grill (broil) until the sugar has melted and the figs have softened.

Spoon the porridge into bowls, pour on a little milk, then divide the figs and the caramel sauce among the bowls. For the final touch, add a dollop of thick cream.
Serves 4.

Porridge is a wonderful winter warmer, particularly when teamed with soft, ripe figs and caramel sauce.

Flatcakes are a little different from run-of-the-mill pancakes. Because they are more substantial, they are ideal to serve for a special brunch.

ginger and ricotta flatcakes with honeycomb

150 g (1 cup) wholemeal flour
2 tbs caster (superfine) sugar
2 tsp baking powder
2 tsp ground ginger
55 g (1 cup) flaked coconut, toasted
4 eggs, separated
500 g (1 lb 2 oz) ricotta
310 ml (1¼ cups) milk
4 bananas, sliced
200 g (7 oz) fresh honeycomb,
broken into large pieces

Sift the flour, sugar, baking powder and ginger into a bowl. Stir in the coconut and make a little dip in the centre. Add the combined egg yolks, 350 g (12 oz) of the ricotta and all of the milk. Mix until you have a smooth batter.

Now beat the egg whites into a billowy cloud of soft peaks, then fold them into the flatcake mixture — this will make a beautifully light batter.

Heat a frying pan and brush lightly with a little melted butter or oil. Pour 3 tablespoons of the batter into the pan and swirl gently to create an even flatcake. Cook over low heat until bubbles form on the surface, then flip it over and cook the other side until golden. To keep your flatcakes warm, you may like to stack them on a plate, covered with a foil tent, in a moderate oven while you cook the rest.

Stack three flatcakes on a serving plate (best if warmed) and top with a generous dollop of ricotta, some sliced banana and a large piece of fresh honeycomb.
Serves 4.

cheesy cornbread with creamy scrambled eggs

For the cornbread:
155 g (1¼ cups) self-raising flour
1 tbs caster (superfine) sugar
2 tsp baking powder
110 g (¾ cup) fine polenta (cornmeal)
60 g (½ cup) grated Cheddar cheese
25 g (½ cup) chopped mixed herbs
(we used chives, dill and parsley)
2 eggs
250 ml (1 cup) buttermilk
4 tbs macadamia or olive oil

For the scrambled eggs:
6 eggs
125 ml (½ cup) cream
small basil leaves

Sift the flour, sugar, baking powder and 1 teaspoon salt into a bowl. Add the polenta, cheese, herbs, eggs, buttermilk and oil and mix together. Spoon the mixture into a lightly greased 20 cm x 10 cm (8 inch x 4 inch) loaf tin and bake in a 180°C (350°F/Gas 4) oven until a skewer comes out clean, about 45 minutes. Remove from the tin.

To make the scrambled eggs, whisk together the eggs and cream and season with salt and pepper. Pour the mixture into a non-stick frying pan and cook over low heat, stirring occasionally until the egg is just set — if you can resist stirring too much, you'll be rewarded with smooth, creamy eggs. Serve the scrambled eggs with generously buttered cornbread. Sprinkle with basil leaves. Serves 4.

A weekend breakfast should be a long and lazy affair accompanied by steaming coffee, freshly squeezed orange juice and a big pile of the weekend papers.

These little fritters are so good that it's hard to resist eating them one by one as they come out of the pan.

corn and sweet potato fritters

For the dressing:
250 g (1 cup) thick natural yoghurt
3 tbs chopped coriander (cilantro)
2 tsp oil
1/4 tsp finely grated lime zest
2 tbs lime juice

265 g (11/3 cups) corn kernels
250 g (9 oz) orange sweet potato, coarsely grated
1 small onion, coarsely grated
2 eggs
90 g (1/2 cup) rice flour
2 tsp curry powder
4 tbs oil
thin strips of chilli

The dressing is a cinch — simply combine all the ingredients in a small bowl, then leave it while you move on to the fritters.

For the fritters, put the corn kernels, sweet potato, onion, eggs, flour and curry powder in a bowl. Now get in there with your hands and mix it all together.

Heat 11/2 tablespoons of the oil in a large frying pan. Using a tablespoon of the batter each time, form six rough patties and cook them until golden, about 5 minutes. Drain on paper towels and keep warm while you do the same with the rest of the batter. You should end up with 12 fritters.

Heat the rest of the oil in a frying pan and briefly cook the chilli over medium heat until you have thin, crispy strips.

Spoon the dressing on the piping hot fritters, garnish with chilli and serve with plenty of serviettes (paper napkins).
Serves 4 as a snack.

garlicky winey prawns

20 large raw prawns (shrimp)
3 tbs olive oil
85 g (3 oz) butter
half a red chilli, finely chopped
10 garlic cloves, crushed
3 tbs white wine
3 tbs chopped parsley

Peel and devein the prawns, but leave the tails on — they look much more handsome with the tails intact. Pour the oil into a large frying pan. Now add the butter, chilli and half the garlic and cook for a few minutes, stirring all the time.

Add the prawns and then sprinkle with the rest of the garlic. Cook until the prawns turn pink — about 3 minutes. Now turn the prawns over, splash in the wine and cook for another 4 minutes. Sprinkle in the parsley, season well with salt and pepper and serve with plenty of crusty bread to soak up the deliciously aromatic juices.
Serves 4 as a starter.

Some foods need to be savoured in all their glorious simplicity, with just a touch of this or a dab of that to enhance the flavours.

Some meals make it very easy to contemplate vegetarianism, and with such a variety of things to crunch on, this dish is definitely one of them.

stir-fried mixed vegetables

2 tbs soy sauce
1 tsp fish sauce
1 tbs oyster sauce
3 tbs vegetable stock
1/2 tsp grated palm sugar or
soft brown sugar
2 tbs oil
4 spring onions (scallions), cut into
3 cm (1 1/4 inch) lengths
3 garlic cloves, crushed
1 red chilli, seeded and sliced
70 g (2 1/2 oz) button mushrooms, quartered
100 g (3 1/2 oz) Chinese cabbage,
roughly chopped
150 g (5 1/2 oz) snow peas
150 g (5 1/2 oz) cauliflower, cut into
small florets
150 g (5 1/2 oz) broccoli, cut into
small florets
chopped coriander (cilantro) leaves

Start by preparing your stir-fry sauce — you'll add it towards the end. Mix together the soy sauce, fish sauce, oyster sauce, stock and palm sugar and stir until the sugar has dissolved.

Heat a wok until very hot, add the oil and swirl it around the side of the wok. Add the spring onion, garlic and chilli and stir-fry briefly without burning. Throw in the mushrooms and cabbage and stir-fry for a minute. Pour in your stir-fry sauce, then add the snow peas, cauliflower and broccoli and cook until the vegetables are tender, only 2 minutes or so. Garnish with the coriander leaves and serve with plenty of steamed rice. Serves 6.

chicken with thai basil

1 tbs fish sauce
1 tbs oyster sauce
2 tsp lime juice
1 tbs grated palm sugar or
soft brown sugar
3 tbs peanut oil
500 g (1 lb 2 oz) chicken breast fillets,
trimmed and cut into thin strips
1 garlic clove, crushed
4 spring onions (scallions), thinly sliced
150 g (5$1/2$ oz) snake beans, trimmed and
cut into 5 cm (2 inch) lengths
2 small red chillies, thinly sliced
35 g ($3/4$ cup) tightly packed Thai basil,
plus a bit extra
2 tbs chopped mint

Most stir-fries have a sauce that adds flavour right at the end. This one is no exception. To make the sauce, combine the fish sauce, oyster sauce, lime juice, palm sugar and 2 tablespoons water. Mix together until the sugar dissolves. Leave until you need it.

Heat a wok over high heat, add 1 tablespoon of the oil and swirl to coat. Cook the chicken in batches until lightly browned and almost cooked, about 4 minutes. You might find you need a little more oil between batches. Scoop the chicken out of the wok and keep warm.

Heat the remaining oil in the wok, then briefly stir-fry the garlic, spring onions, snake beans and chillies until the spring onions are tender. Toss the chicken back into the wok.

Toss in the basil and mint, then add your stir-fry sauce and cook for 1 minute. Garnish with the extra basil and serve with steamed jasmine rice.
Serves 4.

To get the best out of stir-fries, serve them straight away so the smoky flavour from the wok clings to the food.

Just about every region of Italy has its own version of minestrone, so feel free to experiment with the basic recipe to make your own favourite soup.

hearty minestrone with pesto

125 g (4½ oz) dried borlotti beans
3 tbs olive oil
1 large onion, finely chopped
2 garlic cloves, crushed
60 g (2¼ oz) pancetta, finely chopped
1 celery stalk, diced
1 carrot, diced
1 potato, peeled and diced
2 tsp tomato paste (purée)
400 g (14 oz) can chopped tomatoes
6 basil leaves, roughly torn
2 litres (8 cups) chicken or vegetable stock
2 thin zucchini (courgettes), cut into
1.5 cm (5/8 inch) slices
115 g (3/4 cup) shelled peas
60 g (2¼ oz) green beans, cut into
short lengths
85 g (3 oz) silverbeet (Swiss chard), shredded
3 tbs chopped flat-leaf (Italian) parsley
70 g (2½ oz) ditalini or other small pasta

For the pesto:
30 g (1 cup) basil
25 g (1 oz) lightly toasted pine nuts
2 garlic cloves
100 ml (3½ fl oz) olive oil
3 tbs grated Parmesan

Soak the borlotti beans in cold water overnight, then thoroughly drain and rinse them.

Heat the oil in a large deep saucepan, add the onion, garlic and pancetta and cook over low heat, stirring occasionally until tender and soft, about 10 minutes.

Now add the celery, carrot and potato to the pan and cook for 5 minutes before stirring in the tomato paste, tomatoes, basil and drained borlotti beans. Season with pepper. Pour in the stock and bring slowly to the boil. Cover and simmer for 1½ hours, stirring every now and then.

Add the remaining vegetables, parsley and the pasta. Let it simmer away until the vegetables and pasta are *al dente* — 10 minutes at the most. Season if you think it needs it.

Now for the pesto. Combine the basil, pine nuts and garlic with a pinch of salt in a food processor. Blitz until finely chopped. With the motor running, slowing pour in the olive oil. Scoop into a bowl and stir in the Parmesan and some pepper. Dollop onto the soup. Serves 6.

rich snapper pies

2 tbs olive oil
4 onions, thinly sliced
375 ml (1 1/2 cups) fish stock
875 ml (3 1/2 cups) cream
1 kg (2 lb 4 oz) skinless snapper fillets,
cut into large pieces
2 teaspoons truffle-flavoured oil
(optional)
2 sheets of ready-rolled puff pastry,
thawed
1 egg, lightly beaten

The first step is to lightly caramelize the onions. To do this, heat the oil in a deep frying pan, add the onions and stir over medium heat for about 20 minutes.

Pour in the fish stock, bring to the boil and cook until the liquid has nearly evaporated, about 10 minutes. Stir in the cream and bring to the boil. Now reduce the heat and let it simmer away until the liquid has reduced by half — it will need 20 minutes or so.

Scoop half the sauce into four 500 ml (2 cup) ramekins. Put some fish pieces in each ramekin and then dollop on the rest of the sauce. Add 1/2 teaspoon truffle oil to each pie. Cut the pastry sheets into rounds that are slightly larger than the tops of the ramekins. Brush the edges of the pastry with a little of the egg, then use the egg as a kind of glue to keep the pastry rounds in place on the ramekins. Now brush the pastry tops with the remaining beaten egg so you'll get a professional looking finish to your pies. Bake in a 220°C (425°F/Gas 7) oven until the tops are beautifully puffed up and the filling is steaming hot.
Serves 4.

The merest hint of truffle oil adds an exquisite earthy aroma and flavour.

These pot pies are so sublime that you'll never be tempted to buy a pie for lunch again.

chicken and leek pot pies

2 tbs olive oil
500 g (1 lb 2 oz) chicken thighs,
cut into 2 cm (3/4 inch) dice
60 g (2 1/4 oz) butter
1 leek, thinly sliced
3 garlic cloves, crushed
3 tbs dry white wine
2 tbs plain (all-purpose) flour
250 ml (1 cup) chicken stock
125 ml (1/2 cup) cream
2 tsp chopped thyme
2 tbs chopped parsley
2 sheets puff pastry
1 egg, lightly beaten

Fry the chicken in two batches over high heat until lightly browned but not cooked all the way through, about 4 minutes. Remove from the pan with a slotted spoon.

Melt the butter in the same pan and when it's sizzling, cook the leek and garlic over low heat until softened but not browned. Return the chicken to the pan, splash in the wine and boil until nearly all the wine has evaporated, leaving just the flavour. Sprinkle the flour over the top, stir briefly, then add the stock, cream and thyme. Reduce the heat and simmer gently until the chicken is tender and the sauce has reduced and thickened, about 20 minutes. Season to taste, remove from the heat and cool. Stir in the parsley.

Divide the mixture among four 315 ml (1 1/4 cup) ramekins. Cut four 12 cm (4 3/4 inch) rounds from the pastry, brush the ramekin rims with a little beaten egg, then place the pastry lids on top. Press the rims down firmly to seal. If you're feeling artistic, cut out pastry scraps to decorate the tops. Brush with egg and cut three steam holes in each pie with a knife. Bake on the bottom shelf of a 200°C (400°F/Gas 6) oven until the pastry is golden. Serves 4.

beef pie

2 tbs oil
1 kg (2 lb 4 oz) trimmed chuck steak, cut into cubes
1 large onion, chopped
1 large carrot, finely chopped
2 garlic cloves, crushed
2 tbs plain (all-purpose) flour
250 ml (1 cup) beef stock
2 tsp thyme
1 tbs Worcestershire sauce
750 g (1 lb 10 oz) ready-rolled shortcrust pastry
1 egg yolk
1 tbs milk

Heat half the oil in a large frying pan and brown the meat in batches. Remove from the pan. Heat the remaining oil, add the onion, carrot and garlic and brown over medium heat. Return the meat to the pan and stir in the flour. Cook for a minute, then take off the hob and slowly stir in the stock, mixing the flour in well. Add the thyme and Worcestershire sauce and bring to the boil. Season.

Reduce the heat to very low, cover and simmer until the meat is tender — this could take up to 2 hours. During the last 15 minutes, remove the lid so the sauce thickens. Cool completely.

Divide the pastry in half and roll out one piece between two sheets of baking paper until large enough to line a lightly greased 23 cm (9 inch) pie plate. Line the plate, fill with the cold filling and roll out the remaining pastry to cover the pie plate. Brush the pastry edges with water. Lay the pastry over the pie and gently press or pinch to seal. Trim any excess pastry. Cut a few steam holes in the top of the pastry. Beat together the egg yolk and milk and brush over the top of the pie. Bake in a 200°C (400°F/Gas 6) oven until the pastry is golden, about 30 minutes.
Serves 6.

A chunky, meaty homemade pie is, without a doubt, one of the better things in life. Serve it with a big bowl of creamy garlic mash for the ultimate winter warmer.

sausages with thick onion sauce

1 tbs olive oil
8 thick sausages (pork or bratwurst)

For the onion sauce:
40 g (1 1/2 oz) butter
3 onions, thinly sliced
2 garlic cloves, crushed
1 tbs plain (all-purpose) flour
500 ml (2 cups) beef stock
125 ml (1/2 cup) dry white wine
2 tsp Dijon mustard
3 tsp soft brown sugar
1 tsp chopped thyme

Heat the oil in a large frying pan and fry the sausages over medium heat until browned on all sides, 5 minutes or so. Remove to a plate and keep warm while you make the sauce.

To make the onion sauce, melt the butter in the same frying pan, add the onions and slowly cook over low heat until soft and golden — this will take about 20 minutes. Stir the onions every now and then. Add the garlic and cook for 30 seconds. Stir in the flour and briefly cook over low heat to brown. Take the pan off the hob and gradually pour in the stock and wine. Return to the heat and bring to the boil. Stir in the mustard, sugar and thyme, then reduce the heat and simmer gently, stirring occasionally until nice and thick. Season with pepper.

Add the sausages to the sauce and simmer, stirring until cooked through, 10 minutes.

Serve the sausages and sauce over a bed of mashed potato with steamed vegetables. Serves 4.

This is the sort of dinner you want to eat when it's too cold to go out and there's a good movie on the television. Make sure you've got some chocolate for dessert.

The word 'tagine' refers not only to the classic stews of Morocco but also to the special earthenware dishes, with their distinctive pointed tops, in which the stews are traditionally cooked.

lamb tagine with quince

1.5 kg (3 lb 5 oz) lamb shoulder, cut into 3 cm (1¼ inch) pieces
2 large onions, diced
½ tsp ground ginger
½ tsp cayenne pepper
¼ tsp pulverized saffron threads
1 tsp ground coriander
1 cinnamon stick
25 g (½ cup) roughly chopped coriander (cilantro)
40 g (1½ oz) butter
500 g (1 lb 2 oz) quinces, peeled, cored and quartered
100 g (3½ oz) dried apricots
coriander (cilantro) sprigs

Put the lamb in a heavy-based, flameproof casserole dish and add half of the diced onion, the ginger, cayenne pepper, saffron, ground coriander, cinnamon stick, coriander and some salt and pepper. Cover with cold water and bring to the boil over medium heat. Lower the heat and let it simmer away, partly covered, for an hour.

While the lamb is cooking, melt the butter in a heavy-based frying pan and cook the rest of the onion and the quinces over medium heat until lightly golden, about 15 minutes.

Add the quinces and apricots to the lamb, then let simmer away for another half hour. Taste the sauce and season with salt and pepper if you think it needs it. Scoop into a warm serving dish and sprinkle with coriander sprigs. Delicious served with couscous or rice. Serves 4–6.

tomatoey osso bucco

10 pieces of veal shank, about 4 cm
(1¹/₂ inch) thick
plain (all-purpose) flour, seasoned with
salt and pepper
3 tbs olive oil
60 g (2¹/₄ oz) butter
1 garlic clove
1 small carrot, finely chopped
1 large onion, finely chopped
half a celery stalk, finely chopped
250 ml (1 cup) dry white wine
375 ml (1¹/₂ cups) veal or chicken stock
400 g (14 oz) can chopped tomatoes
bouquet garni

Keep the pieces of veal shank neat and tidy by tying a piece of string around the edge, then dust with the seasoned flour. Get a big, heavy saucepan that will fit all the shanks in a single layer. Now heat the oil, butter and garlic in it before you add the shanks. Cook them until well browned, about 15 minutes. Lift the shanks out of the saucepan and set aside. Discard the garlic.

Add the carrot, onion and celery to the pan and cook over medium heat for about 5 minutes, without browning. Increase the heat to high, splash in the wine and cook for a few minutes to evaporate the alcohol. Add the stock, tomatoes and bouquet garni. Season.

Return the veal shanks to the saucepan, standing them up in a single layer. Cover the pan, reduce the heat and simmer for an hour, or until the meat is tender enough to cut it with a fork.

If you like a thick, rich sauce, take the shanks out of the pan and increase the heat. Boil the sauce until it's thick enough for you, then return the veal to the pan to reheat. Discard the bouquet garni and season to taste. Serves 4.

This is one of those full-flavoured hearty stews that you make by throwing everything into the one pot, then cooking it to perfection.

Cut off a big slab of this pud, pour on some of the sauce and serve with generous scoops of ice cream that will melt into runny, gooey pools of cream.

self-saucing chocolate pudding

knob of unsalted butter, melted
50 g (1 3/4 oz) unsalted butter, chopped
70 g (2 1/2 oz) good-quality dark chocolate, chopped
125 ml (1/2 cup) milk
125 g (1 cup) self-raising flour
4 tbs cocoa powder
145 g (2/3 cup) caster (superfine) sugar
1 egg, lightly beaten
115 g (1/2 cup) soft brown sugar
icing (confectioners') sugar

Lightly grease a 2 litre (8 cup) ovenproof dish with the melted butter. Put the chopped butter, chocolate and milk in a small saucepan, and stir over medium heat until the butter and chocolate have melted into a glossy sauce. Take the pan off the hob and leave it to cool slightly.

Sift together the flour and 2 tablespoons of cocoa, and add to the chocolate mixture with the caster sugar and the egg, stirring until just combined. Spoon into the prepared dish.

Sift the remaining cocoa evenly over the top of the pudding and sprinkle with the brown sugar. Pour 560 ml (2 1/4 cups) boiling water over the back of a spoon (this stops the water making big holes in the cake mixture) over the top of the pudding. Now bake in a 180°C (350°F/Gas 4) oven until the pudding is firm to the touch, about 40 minutes. Leave for a couple of minutes before dusting with icing sugar. Serve with lashings of cream or generous scoops of vanilla ice cream. Serves 6.

really special chocolate croissant pudding

4 croissants, torn into pieces
100 g (3 1/2 oz) dark chocolate, chopped into pieces
4 eggs
4 tbs caster (superfine) sugar
250 ml (1 cup) milk
250 ml (1 cup) cream
1/2 tsp grated orange zest
4 tbs orange juice
2 tbs roughly chopped hazelnuts

Lightly grease the base and side of a 20 cm (8 inch) deep-sided cake tin and line the bottom of the tin with baking paper. Toss the croissant pieces into the tin, then scatter with bits of chocolate.

Beat the eggs and sugar together until pale and creamy.

Heat the milk and cream in a saucepan to almost boiling, then remove from the heat. Gradually pour it into the egg mixture, stirring constantly. Add the orange zest and juice and stir well. Slowly pour the mixture over the croissants, allowing the liquid to be absorbed before adding more.

Sprinkle the top with the hazelnuts and bake in a 180°C (350°F/Gas 4) oven until a skewer comes out clean when inserted in the centre — it will need about 45 minutes. Cool for 10 minutes. Run a knife around the edge, then turn out and invert. Scoop out some pudding and serve warm (hint: it's wonderful with lots of cream).
Serves 6–8.

Who says croissants are just for breakfast? And why eat them with just a little butter and jam when you can smother them in chocolate and cream? The proof is definitely in the pudding.

The contrasting textures of the sweet, fresh, mushy rhubarb and the buttery, bitty, crumble topping will have you back for seconds.

rhubarb and berry crumble

850 g (1 lb 14 oz) rhubarb, cut into
2.5 cm (1 inch) lengths
150 g (5½ oz) blackberries
1 tsp grated orange zest
1 cup (230 g) caster (superfine) sugar
1 cup (125 g) plain (all-purpose) flour
1 cup (100 g) ground almonds
½ tsp ground ginger
150 g (5½ oz) chilled unsalted butter,
cut into cubes

Bring a saucepan of water to the boil over high heat, add the rhubarb and cook until just tender. Drain well and combine with the berries, orange zest and 4 tablespoons of the caster sugar. Taste and add a little more sugar if you think it needs it. Spoon the fruit mixture into a lightly greased deep, 1.5 litre (6 cup) ovenproof dish

To make the topping, combine the flour, ground almonds, ginger and the remaining sugar. Rub the butter into the flour mixture with your fingertips until it resembles coarse breadcrumbs. Sprinkle the crumble mix over the fruit, pressing lightly. Don't press it down too firmly, or it will become flat and dense.

Sit the dish on a baking tray and bake in a 180°C (350°F/Gas 4) oven until you have a golden topping and a bubbling fruit base. Try to resist digging in for a few minutes to let it cool slightly, then serve with cream or vanilla ice cream.
Serves 4.

Perfect sipped in front of a roaring fire while you cosy up with a friend.

mulled wine

12 cloves, pushed into 2 oranges
2 lemons, thinly sliced
3 tbs sugar
1 whole nutmeg, grated,
4 cinnamon sticks
750 ml (3 cups) full-bodied red wine

Put the oranges, lemon slices, sugar, nutmeg, cinnamon and 500 ml (2 cups) water in a saucepan. Bring to the boil, then reduce the heat, cover the pan and simmer for 20 minutes. Leave to cool, then strain into a bowl.

Pour the spicy liquid into a clean pan, add the wine and heat until almost boiling — don't boil or the alcohol will evaporate (and you don't want that). Serve in heatproof glasses. Serves 6.

Some people swear by the medicinal properties of a hot toddy ... but who needs an excuse to drink it?

hot toddy

1 tbs soft brown sugar
4 slices of lemon
4 cinnamon sticks,
12 whole cloves
125 ml (1/2 cup) whisky

Put the sugar, lemon slices, cinnamon, cloves, whisky and 1 litre (4 cups) boiling water in a heatproof jug. Give a good stir and then let it infuse for a few minutes.

Now strain into a serving jug. Taste a little and see if it needs more sugar. Serve in heatproof glasses.
Serves 4.

creamy
food that caresses

Breakfast in a glass or a thick, creamy pick-me-up.

bananarama smoothie

1 large banana, chopped
2 tbs thick natural yoghurt
250 ml (1 cup) milk
honey (optional)
nutmeg

Put the banana, yoghurt and milk in a blender and blitz into a smooth, creamy mixture. Taste a little and add some honey if you think it needs it, then pour into tall glasses. For the final touch, sprinkle with a little nutmeg.
Serves 1.

Serve this chocolatey shake
'50s style in a tall aluminium
container with a stripy straw.

double choc milkshake

250 ml (1 cup) chocolate milk
4 scoops of chocolate ice cream
grated chocolate

Blend the milk and ice cream in a blender until smooth, rich and chocolatey. Pour into chilled glasses and decorate with grated chocolate.
Serves 2.

So much more than a basic mash — sour cream adds a richness that lifts it to the sublime.

no ordinary mashed potato

1 kg (2 lb 4 oz) desiree potatoes, cut into quarters
2–3 tbs butter
185 g (3/4 cup) sour cream

Boil the potato in a large saucepan of water for 12 minutes, or until soft. Drain, then return to the heat, shaking to dry any excess water. Add the butter and sour cream and mash with a potato masher until smooth and lump-free. Season to taste.
Serves 4.

This garlicky cheesy purée has an intriguing glossy texture.

aligot

800 g (1 lb 12 oz) floury potatoes, cut into even-sized pieces
70 g (2^1/$_2$ oz) butter
2 garlic cloves, crushed
3 tbs milk
300 g (10^1/$_2$ oz) Cantal or mild Cheddar cheese, grated

Cook the potatoes in boiling salted water until tender, about 25 minutes. Meanwhile, gently melt the butter and add the garlic.

Mash the potatoes and then sieve to give a smooth purée. Now return to the pan over low heat and add the garlic butter and milk. Mix well and then beat in the cheese, a handful at a time — once it has melted, the mixture will be stretchy and glossy. Season. Serves 4.

Serve the carbonara with plenty of fresh crusty bread to mop up all of the thick, creamy sauce that is lingering in the bottom of your pasta bowl.

spaghetti carbonara

400 g (14 oz) spaghetti
2 eggs
2 egg yolks
60 g (2¼ oz) Parmesan cheese, grated,
plus extra for serving
2 tbs olive oil
30 g (1 oz) butter
2 garlic cloves, bruised
200 g (7 oz) pancetta,
cut into small strips

Cook the pasta in a large saucepan of boiling salted water until *al dente*.

Meanwhile, mix the eggs, egg yolks and Parmesan together in a bowl and season lightly with salt and pepper.

Heat the oil and butter in a large frying pan and when it's sizzling, cook the garlic and pancetta until the pancetta is crisp. Discard the garlic when it becomes golden — it will have done its job by adding a delicate garlicky fragrance.

Once the spaghetti is cooked, drain it well and add it to the frying pan and toss well. Take the pan off the hob, then pour on the egg mixture — the heat of the pasta will cook the egg and you'll end up with a sauce that caresses every strand of your spaghetti. Serve immediately, with lots of grated Parmesan and a little black pepper. Serves 4.

indian butter chicken

2 cm (3/4 inch) piece of fresh ginger, roughly chopped
3 garlic cloves, roughly chopped
70 g (2¹/2 oz) blanched almonds
150 ml (5 fl oz) thick natural yoghurt
¹/2 tsp chilli powder
¹/4 tsp ground cloves
¹/4 tsp ground cinnamon
1 tsp garam masala
4 cardamom pods, lightly crushed
400 g (14 oz) can chopped tomatoes
1 kg (2 lb 4 oz) skinless, boneless chicken thigh fillets, cut into fairly large pieces
5 tbs ghee or clarified butter
1 large onion, thinly sliced
6 tbs finely chopped coriander (cilantro) leaves
4 tbs thick (double/heavy) cream

Make a sort of paste out of the ginger and garlic — either blitz in a food processor or go more traditional with a mortar and pestle. Next, grind the almonds — you'll definitely need a food processor for this. Put the paste and almonds in a bowl along with the yoghurt, chilli powder, cloves, cinnamon, garam masala, cardamom pods, tomato and 1¹/4 teaspoon salt, and blend together with a fork. Add the chicken pieces and smear them thoroughly. Cover and marinate in the fridge for 2 hours, or overnight if you have the time.

Heat the ghee in a deep, heavy-based frying pan, add the onion and fry until softened and brown. Add the chicken mixture and fry for 2 minutes. Mix in the coriander. Now scoop into a shallow baking dish, pour in the cream and stir well.

Bake for an hour in a 180°C (350°F/Gas 4) oven. If the top is browning too quickly, cover with a piece of foil. Leave to rest for 10 minutes — you'll find that the oil will rise to the surface. Just before serving, sit the dish under a hot grill (broiler) to brown the top. Once that's done, slightly tip the dish and spoon off any extra oil that rose to the top.
Serves 6.

If India has a comfort food, this would have to be it. It's guaranteed to soothe all ills with its combination of melt-in-the-mouth chicken pieces cooked in a fragrant, creamy sauce.

When it's too hot for coffee or tea, but you can't survive without a caffeine hit, coffee gelato comes to the rescue.

coffee gelato

5 egg yolks
115 g (1/2 cup) sugar
500 ml (2 cups) milk
125 ml (1/2 cup) freshly made espresso
1 tbs Tia Maria

Whisk the egg yolks and half the sugar together until you have a pale and creamy mass. Pour the milk and coffee into a saucepan, add the remaining sugar and bring to the boil. Now pour it into the egg mixture and whisk together. Pour back into the saucepan and cook over low heat, stirring continuously until the mixture is thick enough to coat the back of a wooden spoon, being careful that the custard doesn't boil.

Strain the custard into a bowl and cool over ice before stirring in the Tia Maria. To turn the custard into ice cream, you can use an ice-cream maker or the traditional method. If you've got a machine, follow the manufacturer's instructions. Otherwise pour the mixture into a plastic freezer box, cover and freeze. Stir every 30 minutes with a whisk during freezing to break up the ice crystals and give a better texture. Keep in the freezer until ready to serve.
Serves 6.

crème brûlée

750 ml (3 cups) cream
2 vanilla beans
8 egg yolks
115 g (1/2 cup) sugar
3 tsp sugar

Heat the cream and vanilla beans in a saucepan until almost boiling. Take the pan off the hob for half an hour so the vanilla can impart its fragrance to the cream. Lift the beans out.

Beat or whisk the egg yolks and sugar in a large bowl until you have a thick, pale mass. Stir in your vanilla cream, then pour the whole lot into a clean pan over low heat and stir until the mixture thickens slightly — enough to coat the back of a wooden spoon. Don't boil or you will curdle the mixture. Remove from the heat and ladle into six 170 ml (5 1/2 fl oz) ramekins. Cover with plastic wrap and refrigerate for at least 3 hours, or overnight if you can spare the time.

Just before serving, preheat the grill (broiler) to very hot. Sprinkle a layer of sugar about 3 mm (1/8 inch) thick over the surface of the brûlées. Sit the ramekins in a large baking dish and pack ice around the sides to prevent the custards being heated. Either sit under the grill or wave a mini blowtorth over the sugar until it caramelizes into a sheet.

Chill the brûlées until you serve them but not for longer than an hour or the crust will soften. Serves 6.

If you want to add an element of drama to the proceedings, try deftly wielding a blowtorch over each custard to caramelize the sugar topping.

There are some occasions where a single chocolate mousse will do, and others where nothing but a double whammy will satisfy.

doubly good chocolate mousse

250 g (9 oz) white chocolate, melted
90 g (3¼ oz) good-quality dark
chocolate, chopped
15 g (½ oz) unsalted butter
2 eggs, separated
250 ml (1 cup) cream, whipped

The first step is to make white chocolate cups to hold the mousse. Cut some baking paper into six 16 cm (6½ inch) squares. Working with one sheet at a time, spread six circles of melted white chocolate onto the paper. Drape each piece over the rim of a glass or mould, chocolate-side up. When set, carefully peel away the baking paper, then refrigerate your chocolate cups.

To make the mousse, melt the dark chocolate with the butter in a double saucepan or zap in the microwave for 1 minute on High (100%), stirring after 30 seconds. Whisk in the egg yolks and allow to cool. Fold in half the cream. Beat the egg whites until soft peaks form, then lightly fold into the mousse until well combined. Fold in the remaining cream to make a swirled pattern. Spoon the mousse into the chocolate cups and chill for several hours before serving.
Serves 6.

new york cheesecake

60 g (1/2 cup) self-raising flour
125 g (1 cup) plain (all-purpose) flour
3 tbs caster (superfine) sugar
1 tsp grated lemon zest
80 g (2 3/4 oz) unsalted butter, chopped
1 egg
whipped cream, for serving

For the filling:
750 g (1 lb 10 oz) cream cheese, softened
230 g (1 cup) caster (superfine) sugar
3 tbs plain (all-purpose) flour
2 tsp grated orange zest
2 tsp grated lemon zest
4 eggs
170 ml (2/3 cup) cream, whipped

Briefly blitz the flours, sugar, lemon zest and butter in a food processor until crumbly. Add the egg and, again, process until the mixture just comes together. Turn out onto a lightly floured surface and gather together into a ball. Refrigerate in plastic wrap for about 20 minutes, or until the dough is firm.

Lightly grease a 23 cm (9 inch) springform tin. Roll out the dough between two sheets of baking paper until large enough to fit the base and side of the tin. Ease into the tin and trim the edges. Cover the pastry with baking paper, then baking beads. Now bake for 10 minutes in a 210°C (415°F/Gas 6–7) oven, then remove the baking paper. Flatten the pastry lightly with the back of a spoon and bake for another 5 minutes. Now leave to cool.

To make the filling, reduce the oven to 150°C (300°F/Gas 2). Beat the cream cheese, sugar, flour and zests until smooth. Beat in the eggs, one at a time, then the cream. Pour into the pastry base and bake until almost set, about 1 1/2 hours. Now for some patience — turn off the oven and leave to cool with the door ajar. When cool, chill completely in the fridge. Decorate with whipped cream, then serve. Serves 10–12.

Fortunately, there are better ways to indulge your cheesecake craving than with a slice of one of those awful, bright red, jelly-topped creations. Instead, go for the real thing — enticingly rich and dense.

Italian 'cooked cream', panna cotta is a silky smooth custard. A ruby red berry sauce marries beautifully with this sweet, milky white dessert.

panna cotta with ruby sauce

750 ml (3 cups) cream
3 tsp gelatine
1 vanilla bean
4 tbs caster (superfine) sugar

For the ruby sauce:
230 g (1 cup) caster (superfine) sugar
1 cinnamon stick
125 g (½ punnet) raspberries (or use frozen ones if fresh aren't in season)
125 ml (½ cup) good-quality red wine

Spoon 3 tablespoons of the cream into a small bowl, then sprinkle the gelatine in an even layer over the surface and leave it to go soft and spongy.

Pour the rest of the cream into a saucepan with the vanilla bean and sugar and heat gently while stirring, until almost boiling. Remove from the heat and whisk the gelatine into the cream mixture until dissolved. Now ladle the creamy mixture into six 150 ml (5 fl oz) ramekins or moulds and chill until set, about 2 hours. Unmould by wiping a cloth dipped in hot water over the mould and upending it onto a plate.

While the panna cotta is being chilled, move on to the ruby sauce. Stir the sugar with 250 ml (1 cup) water in a pan over medium heat until the sugar has completely dissolved (do not allow to boil). Add the cinnamon stick and simmer for 5 minutes. Add the raspberries and wine and boil rapidly for 5 minutes. Remove the cinnamon stick and push the sauce through a sieve — you won't need the seeds. Cool, then pop in the fridge to chill before serving with the panna cotta. Serves 6.

salty
tastes that linger

Get your weekend off to a good start with a generous stack of fritters. Perfect on those mornings when your memories of the night before are a little hazy …

corn fritters with crispy prosciutto

8 ripe Roma (plum) tomatoes, halved
140 g (^{1}/2 cup) spicy tomato chutney
185 g (1^1/2 cups) self-raising flour
75 g (^{1}/2 cup) coarse polenta (cornmeal)
1 tsp sugar
1 egg, lightly beaten
375 ml (1^1/2 cups) buttermilk
2 corn cobs, kernels removed, or
410 g (14 oz) can corn kernels, drained
4 spring onions (scallions), chopped
2 tbs snipped chives
3 tbs grated Parmesan cheese
4 tbs olive oil
12 thin slices of prosciutto
chervil leaves

Lay the tomatoes on a non-stick baking tray, sprinkle with sea salt and freshly ground black pepper and bake in a 200°C (400°F/Gas 6) oven until tender, about 30 minutes. Now chop the tomatoes and mix with the chutney.

Sift the flour, polenta and sugar into a large bowl and whisk in the combined egg and buttermilk until you have a smooth batter. Fold in the corn, spring onions, chives and Parmesan — try to get them evenly divided through the batter. Taste a little, then add as much salt and pepper as you think it needs.

Heat the oil in a non-stick frying pan and drop about 3 tablespoons of batter per fritter into the pan. Now fry the fritters for a couple of minutes — you'll know they are ready to turn over when bubbles burst on the surface. Cook the other side until golden. Continue cooking the fritters until all the batter is used up. Keep the cooked fritters warm — stack them on a plate in a low oven.

For the final step, cook the prosciutto until crispy. Serve stacks of fritters drizzled with tomato chutney and topped with prosciutto and chervil leaves.
Serves 4.

smoked salmon bagels

4 plain or rye bagels
100 g (3¹/₂ oz) Neufchâtel cream cheese
200 g (7 oz) sliced smoked salmon
2 spring onions (scallions), chopped
2 Roma (plum) tomatoes, finely chopped
2 tbs baby capers
2 tbs finely chopped dill
2 tbs lemon juice
1 tbs extra virgin olive oil

Cut the bagels in half across the middle and slather the base with cream cheese. Top with the smoked salmon.

Put the spring onions, tomatoes, capers, dill, lemon juice and olive oil in a bowl and mix them all together. Pile this mixture onto the salmon and serve.
Serves 4.

New Yorkers can buy filled bagels on every corner. The rest of us need to make our own. Buy glossy, dense, chewy bagels and fill them with cream cheese and smoked salmon for your own Big Apple moment.

mediterranean blt

4 small vine-ripened tomatoes, halved
1 head of garlic, halved
1 tbs extra virgin olive oil
sea salt
3 tbs basil leaves
1 loaf of Italian wood-fired bread
8 slices of provolone cheese
8 slices of mortadella
120 g (1 bunch) rocket (arugula)
extra virgin olive oil, extra
balsamic vinegar

Put the tomatoes and garlic in a roasting tin and drizzle with the oil. Sprinkle with sea salt and freshly ground black pepper and roast in a 200°C (400°F/Gas 6) oven until the garlic is soft and fragrant and the tomatoes are slightly dried — say 40 minutes. Add the basil leaves and pop back in the oven for another 5 minutes so the leaves become crisp.

Cut four thick slices from the loaf of bread and lightly toast on both sides. Peel the roasted garlic cloves and spread half onto the toast — the flavour will be nice and mild. Top with the provolone, mortadella, rocket, crispy basil and roasted tomatoes. Smear the rest of the garlic over the top, drizzle with oil and vinegar, then serve while nice and hot.
Serves 4.

Something glorious has happened to the sandwich in recent years ... with any number of breads to choose from and a variety of sophisticated toppings, it's become a meal to be appreciated and savoured.

This makes a fabulous weekend lunch when you need to rejuvenate your tastebuds with something fresh and sharp.

spaghettini with asparagus and rocket

100 ml (3¹/₂ fl oz) extra virgin olive oil
16 thin asparagus spears, cut into
5 cm (2 inch) lengths
375 g (13 oz) spaghettini
120 g (1 bunch) rocket (arugula), shredded
2 small red chillies, finely chopped
2 tsp finely grated lemon zest
1 garlic clove, finely chopped
100 g (1 cup) grated Parmesan cheese
2 tbs lemon juice

The first step is to cook the asparagus — the aim is to cook it without turning it to mush. Bring a large saucepan of water to the boil over medium heat. Add 1 tablespoon of the oil and a pinch of salt to the water and blanch the asparagus for 3–4 minutes. Remove the asparagus with a slotted spoon, and straight away refresh it under cold water so that it doesn't keep cooking. Now drain it and put in a biggish bowl.

Return the water in the pan to a rapid boil and then add the spaghettini. Cook the pasta until *al dente*. Drain and return to the pan.

While the pasta is cooking, add the rocket, chilli, lemon zest, garlic and most of the Parmesan to the asparagus and mix really well — though it's messy, it's easiest if you use your hands.

Add the cheesy asparagus mix to the pasta, pour on the lemon juice and the remaining olive oil and season with salt and freshly ground black pepper. Stir well, then divide among four pasta bowls, sprinkle with the remaining Parmesan and serve.
Serves 4.

antipasto plate

Nowadays, there is such a huge range of ready-made goodies available at delis and supermarkets that a great antipasto plate is no challenge. You can choose a wholly vegetarian selection or provide an array of vegetables, meats and seafood for the most colourful and varied antipasto plate.

Appearance is important, so choose either one large platter or several small plates or bowls — avoid cramming the food together or it will look unappetizing. If the individual foods have different herbs and flavourings, they will probably be best served in individual bowls to prevent a confusion of flavours. Serve plenty of bread and grissini to accompany the antipasto, as well as extra olive oil and lemon wedges for dressing. And, lastly, don't forget some small bowls for olive pits or discarded toothpicks.

Olives and vegetables

Olives are a must — some big fat, juicy Kalamatas, little Ligurian olives, or marinated or plain green olives — take your pick.

Choose from a range of marinated artichoke hearts; sun-dried, oven-roasted or vine-ripened tomatoes; chargrilled red capsicum (pepper); eggplant (aubergine) or zucchini (courgette) slices; marinated mushrooms; roasted caramelized baby onions; and lightly blanched asparagus spears.

Cold meats

No antipasto plate would be complete without cold sliced Italian meats —- among the many are salami, prosciutto, mortadella, ham and pepperoni. Buy the best quality you can afford: the fresher the meat is, the better it will taste. Meat is best served with strong accompaniments such as caperberries and olives, which cut through any fattiness, or with sweet fruit like figs and melon that enhance its flavours. For the maximum visual interest, cut the meat in different ways — some sliced lengthways, some into small rounds, and some cubed. Lay out the meats on a platter, folding some and rolling others. Serve at room temperature — meat taken straight from the fridge will have less flavour.

Seafood

A selection of seafood can really enliven an antipasto platter. Generally all it needs is a sprinkling of lemon juice and chopped parsley (and perhaps a little chopped garlic). There are salty anchovies, tender mussels, calamari rings and chargrilled tuna. If you're buying marinated fish in jars or tins, rinse and pat them dry. When choosing anchovies and sardines, go for those in salt or olive oil rather than vegetable oil. Cooked prawns are best bought in their shells and peeled at home, or buy raw ones and cook them yourself, if you prefer.

Sauces

Provide plenty of sauces for dipping. Choose pesto (traditional basil or sun-dried tomato), sharply piquant tapenade, smooth artichoke purée or rich porcini paste, all of which are great on bread.

Cheese

You might like to include one or two cheeses as part of your antipasto platter. Mozzarella, bocconcini, gorgonzola, fontina, provolone and pecorino are a few examples.

prawn tempura

For the dipping sauce:
2 tbs mirin
3 tbs soy sauce
10 g (1/4 oz) bonito flakes

100 g (3 1/2 oz) tempura flour
150 ml (5 fl oz) ice-cold water
vegetable oil
12 large raw prawns (shrimp), peeled and
deveined, with the tails intact
grated daikon
pickled ginger

Tempura is greatly enhanced with a delicate dipping sauce. To make this, simply put the mirin, soy sauce, bonito flakes and 250 ml (1 cup) water in a saucepan. Bring to the boil, then strain and cool while you prepare the prawns.

Tempura batter is a simple mixture of flour and cold water, and the secret is to use a really light touch — only just whisk in the water (preferably with chopsticks) and don't beat out the lumps.

Dip 3 or 4 prawns (you'll find it easier to cook them if they're cold) into the batter and deep-fry in batches (at a constant 180°C/ 350°F) until crisp and golden. Drain on crumpled paper towels.

Serve with the dipping sauce, a small pile of grated daikon (squeeze it dry after grating) and pickled ginger.
Serves 4 as a starter.

Many supermarkets now stock ingredients such as tempura flour — if yours doesn't, you're sure to find it at an Asian grocery store.

If you're a little squeamish about handling squid, ask your fishmonger to clean and halve the tubes for you. There's no excuse for denying yourself this tasty meal.

salt and pepper squid

1 kg (2 lb 4 oz) baby squid, cleaned and tubes cut in half
250 ml (1 cup) milk
2 tbs lemon juice
2 tbs sea salt
1 1/2 tbs white peppercorns
2 tsp sugar
250 g (2 cups) cornflour (cornstarch)
4 egg whites, lightly beaten
oil
lime wedges

Pat the squid tubes dry. Lay them out on a chopping board with the soft insides facing up, and use a sharp knife to make a fine diamond pattern, taking care not to cut all the way through. Cut the tubes into small rectangles and put them in a bowl. Cover with milk and lemon juice and refrigerate for 15 minutes.

Put the salt, peppercorns and sugar in a mortar and pestle or spice grinder and pound or process to a fine powder. Transfer to a bowl and stir in the cornflour. Dip the squid into the egg white, then toss to coat in the salt-and-pepper flour, shaking off any excess.

Deep-fry the squid in batches until crisp and lightly golden. Serve with lime wedges. Serves 4 as a starter.

peking duck

1 large Chinese roast duck (you'll need to go
to a Chinese roast meats shop)
24 Mandarin pancakes from the roast meat
window of Chinese restaurants, or frozen
from Asian supermarkets
6–8 spring onions (scallions), shredded
half a cucumber, shredded
hoisin or plum sauce

Undoubtedly the best part of Chinese roast duck is the glossy skin, and the idea is that each pancake gets a little duck flesh, as well as a strip of the skin. So, either shred the duck meat into pieces with your fingers or cut it into neat pieces with a large carving knife. Then cut the skin into small strips. Arrange both on a serving plate.

Heat the pancakes, either in a steamer for 5 minutes or in a microwave for about 40 seconds.

Arrange the pancakes, spring onions and cucumber on separate plates. You can either get everyone to make their own pancakes or assemble them yourself. If you're doing them yourself, spread about 1 teaspoon of the hoisin sauce in the centre of a pancake, add a few strips of spring onion, a little cucumber, duck skin and meat, then roll up the pancake and turn up the bottom edge to prevent the contents from falling out.
Serves 6 as a starter.

Part of the fun of this popular Chinese dish is wrapping up each delicious pancake with the right combination of tender meat, glossy skin, sweet plum sauce and crunchy spring onion.

won ton soup

250 g (9 oz) raw minced (ground) prawn (shrimp) meat
250 g (9 oz) lean minced (ground) pork
85 g (3 oz) canned water chestnuts, roughly chopped
1 tsp finely chopped fresh ginger
1 1/2 tbs cornflour (cornstarch), plus a bit extra, for dusting
3 1/2 tbs light soy sauce
3 1/2 tbs Shaoxing rice wine
1 1/2 tsp roasted sesame oil
30 square or round won ton wrappers
1.5 litres (6 cups) chicken stock (home-made will make the world of difference)
450 g (1 lb) spinach, trimmed (optional)
2 spring onions (scallions), green part only, finely chopped

For the filling, put the prawn meat, pork, water chestnuts, ginger, cornflour, 2 teaspoons of the soy sauce, 2 teaspoons of the rice wine, 1/2 teaspoon of the sesame oil and 1/2 teaspoon each of salt and black pepper in a bowl. Mix it together really well — best with your hands.

Now fill the won tons, working one at a time. Put a teaspoon of filling in the centre of a wrapper. Brush the edge of the wrapper with a little water, fold in half (crossways, not diagonally) and then bring the two folded corners together and press firmly — they should look a little like tortellini. Put each fat won ton on a cornflour-dusted tray.

Cook the won tons in a covered saucepan of boiling water until they bubble to the surface — 5 minutes or so. Lift them out with a wire sieve or slotted spoon and divide them among six bowls (evenly, so there will be no fights!).

Pour the stock into a saucepan with the remaining soy sauce, rice wine, sesame oil and a teaspoon of salt and bring to the boil. Add the spinach and cook briefly until just wilted. Pour the hot stock over the won tons and sprinkle with the spring onion.
Serves 6.

Find yourself an Asian grocery store and become a frequent visitor. You'll discover a whole new world of exotic ingredients.

This delicious, simple dish makes the most of some quintessential Italian flavours. The sage permeates the chicken, while the prosciutto keeps the breast meat wonderfully moist.

chicken wrapped in prosciutto and sage

4 chicken breast fillets, trimmed
1 tbs lemon juice
1 tbs olive oil
2 garlic cloves, bruised and halved
3 large sage leaves, shredded
8 slices of prosciutto
16 sage leaves (preferably small to medium)
2 tbs olive oil

The first step here is to marinate the chicken in a fragrant garlicky, herby oil. So pop the chicken in a glass or ceramic dish that's big enough to fit it in a single layer. Now mix together your lemon juice, olive oil, garlic and shredded sage and pour over the chicken. You might need to turn the chicken pieces a few times so they're all covered. Cover and refrigerate for 1 hour.

Throw away the garlic and then lightly season the chicken with salt and pepper. Wrap two slices of prosciutto around each breast fillet, tucking in two sage leaves on the top and two on the bottom as you go. The aim is to keep the sage leaves in place, but to keep part of each leaf visible. Stick in a couple of toothpicks to keep the prosciutto in place. Now gently pound the breasts with your hand to flatten them slightly so they will cook evenly.

Heat the oil in a frying pan over medium heat and cook the chicken until golden and cooked through — about 5 minutes on each side. Leave the chicken to rest for a few minutes, then remove the toothpicks and serve. Delicious with soft polenta (cornmeal) and a fresh green salad.
Serves 4.

beer-battered fish with chunky wedges

For the tartare sauce:
185 g (3/4 cup) whole-egg mayonnaise
3 tbs sour cream
6 gherkins, chopped
2 tbs capers
2 tbs chopped parsley

125 g (1 cup) plain (all-purpose) flour
250 ml (1 cup) chilled beer
oil, for deep-frying
1 kg (2 lb 4 oz) sebago potatoes, peeled and cut into thick wedges
4 coral trout fillets or 8 flathead fillets (depending on their size)

The tartare sauce is a cinch — simply combine all the ingredients in a bowl.

Now for the batter. Sift the flour into a bowl and season generously with sea salt and freshly ground black pepper. Whisk in the beer until you have a smooth, beery batter.

To get the wedges perfectly crunchy and golden, they need to be cooked twice. They won't all fit in the pot at once, so cook them in batches. Deep-fry them until they are lightly golden, then lift them out of the oil with a slotted spoon and drain on crumpled paper towels. Once they are all done, return the wedges to the oil (again, in batches) and cook until they are crisp and golden. Lift out of the oil, then sprinkle with sea salt and keep warm while you cook the fish.

Reheat the oil. Pat the fish fillets dry with paper towels. Coat the fish in the prepared batter and cook in batches in the hot oil for 3–5 minutes, depending on the size and thickness of the fish. Serve with the crunchy wedges and lashings of tartare sauce. Serves 4.

Crisp, beery batter is a perfect blanket for fish. It not only protects the fish, leaving you with tender, flaky flesh, it also adds a flavoursome maltiness.

The magic of a pork roast is in the crispy crackling. It's really easy to achieve great crackling — just massage the joint with plenty of oil and salt before it goes in the oven.

roast pork with crispy crackling

4 kg (9 lb) leg of pork
oil and salt, to rub on the pork

For the gravy:
1 tbs brandy or Calvados
(Calvados is apple brandy)
2 tbs plain (all-purpose) flour
375 ml (1½ cups) chicken stock
125 ml (½ cup) unsweetened apple juice

Score the pork rind with a sharp knife at 2 cm (³/4 inch) intervals. Massage in oil and salt — be generous. Put the pork, with the rind uppermost, on a rack in a large roasting tin.

Add a little water to the roasting tin. Bake in a 250°C (500°F/Gas 9) oven for 30 minutes, or until the rind begins to crackle and bubble. Reduce the heat to 180°C (350°F/Gas 4) and bake for another 2 hours 40 minutes. The pork is cooked if the juices run clear when the flesh is pierced with a fork. Do not cover or the crackling will soften. Leave in a warm place for 10 minutes before carving.

For the gravy, drain off all but 2 tablespoons of the juices from the roasting tin, then put the tin on the hob over medium heat. Add the brandy and stir quickly to lift the sticky juices from the bottom of the tin. Cook for a minute. Remove from the heat, stir in the flour and mix well. Return the tin to the heat and cook for 2 minutes, stirring constantly. Remove from the heat, gradually stir in the stock and apple juice, then return to the heat and cook, stirring constantly, until it thickens. Season. Slice the pork and serve with the crackling and gravy.
Serves 6–8.

the perfect cheese board

A cheese board is an easy way to finish off a fine meal. To create the perfect cheese board, remember that simplicity is the key. Don't clutter your board with too many accompaniments. Choose a crisp pear, some muscatels or a slice of candied citron; one good loaf of bread, some crackers or oatcakes; and not too many cheeses — five should be the absolute maximum.

If you're only having a few people over, choose one perfect cheese — either a whole ripe Brie, a big chunk of Cheddar or (if you know your audience) a ripe, whiffy blue. Add to this a few accompaniments and that's all you need. Paradoxically, having one big piece of cheese looks more generous than buying lots of itty bits of cheese. But if you're serving lots of people, choose a wider selection of cheeses so that there is something for everyone. An example of a well-balanced cheese board would be to choose one of each of the following types of cheese: goat's cheese, semi-soft cheese, soft-rind cheese, blue cheese and hard cheese.

Keep in mind that because cheese should be served at room temperature, you'll need to be around to take it out of the fridge at least 4 hours before you want to serve it, maybe more in cold weather. Present your cheese selection on an attractive board or large platter and enjoy!

Storing cheese

Cheese is a living substance and should be stored carefully until eaten. It needs humidity, yet it must not get wet. Never freeze cheese; store it in a box (not sealed) in the vegetable crisper or lowest part of the fridge.

Never store cheese wrapped in plastic wrap because harmful substances in the plastic can migrate into the food. If you buy it packed in this, remove it immediately and wrap it in waxed paper, aluminium foil or in a cloth cheese bag, then tightly seal the wrapping with sticky tape or rubber bands. If the cheese comes properly wrapped by the cheesemaker, use that wrapping.

Prefectly ripe cheese

Pre-packed cheese or cheese packed in containers will have a 'best before' or 'use-by' date. It is assumed that, in the right conditions, the cheese will continue to mature up until the 'use-by' date and from then on it will start to deteriorate. When buying packaged cheese, check the date to make sure it will be ready on the day you want it. This means that if you are shopping from the supermarket you may have to buy your cheese some days in advance to get it as close to the optimum 'use-by' date as possible. Specialized cheese shops make it easy for you — they will look after the maturing process and will sell you cheese for the day you want to eat it.

Cutting the cheese

When it comes to cutting your cheese, the idea is to cut it in such a way that each part of the cheese, from the rind to the heart, can be enjoyed. So, for wheels of cheese, cut slices as though you were eating a pie. For square cheese, cut generous wedges or cut into thin slices.

To cut the cheese, ideally, you should use a cheese knife. There are a couple of versions of cheese knife, but all have a forked tip, which skewers pieces of cheese and helps lift it onto a waiting cracker or chunk of bread. The most useful type also has a serrated edge to help it cope with hard cheese and has holes in the blade so that soft cheeses don't stick to it.

sugary
sweet surrender

high-top cappuccino and white-choc muffins

3 tbs instant espresso coffee powder
1 tbs boiling water
310 g (2^1/$_2$ cups) self-raising flour
115 g (^{1}/$_2$ cup) caster (superfine) sugar
2 eggs, lightly beaten
375 ml (1^1/$_2$ cups) buttermilk
1 tsp vanilla essence
150 g (5^1/$_2$ oz) unsalted butter, melted
100 g (3^1/$_2$ oz) white chocolate, roughly chopped
30 g (1 oz) unsalted butter, extra
3 tbs brown sugar

Cut eight lengths of baking paper and roll into 8 cm (3 inch) high cylinders to fit into eight 125 ml (^{1}/$_2$-cup) capacity ramekins. When in place in the ramekins, secure the cylinders with string and put all the ramekins onto a baking tray.

Dissolve the coffee in boiling water and then allow to cool.

Sift the flour and sugar into a bowl. Combine the eggs, buttermilk, vanilla, melted butter, white chocolate and the coffee mixture and mix roughly with the dry ingredients. Spoon the mixture into each cylinder. Heat the extra butter and brown sugar and stir until the sugar dissolves. Spoon this mixture onto each muffin and gently swirl into the muffin using a skewer. Bake for 25–30 minutes in a 200°C (400°F/Gas 6) oven until risen and cooked when tested with a skewer.
Makes 8.

Whip up these sophisticated little cakes in minutes, then serve them fresh from the oven with a scoop of ice cream for dessert, or nibble on one with your morning espresso.

pavlova with fresh fruit

4 egg whites, at room temperature
230 g (1 cup) caster (superfine) sugar
375 ml (1½ cups) cream, whipped
1 banana, sliced
125 g (½ punnet) raspberries
125 g (½ punnet) blueberries

Line a baking tray with baking paper. Mark a 20 cm (8 inch) circle on the paper to help you keep a nice, neat pavlova — turn the paper over so the pencil mark is on the bottom.

For a successful pavlova, you'll need a spotlessly clean, dry stainless steel or glass bowl. Put the egg whites in the bowl and beat them slowly into a frothy foam. Now increase the speed until the bubbles in the foam become small and evenly-sized. When at last you have stiff peaks, add the sugar gradually, beating constantly after each addition, until the mixture is thick and glossy and all the sugar has dissolved.

Spread your glossy clouds onto your drawn circle. Now run a flat-bladed knife around the edge and over the top, then run it up the edge of the mixture, all the way around, to make furrows. This will strengthen the pavlova and make it look gorgeous.

Bake for 40 minutes in a 150°C (300°F/Gas 2) oven until pale and crisp. Turn off the oven and cool the pavlova in the oven with the door ajar. When cold, use your decorating talents with the cream and fruit.
Serves 6–8.

A good meringue should be light, flaky and frivolous with a crisp outer shell coating the deliciously gooey centre — the perfect base for a creamy, fruity topping.

almond friands

150 g (5¹/2 oz) unsalted butter
90 g (1 cup) flaked almonds
4 tbs plain (all-purpose) flour
165 g (1¹/3 cups) icing (confectioners') sugar
5 egg whites
icing (confectioners') sugar, extra, to dust

Melt the butter in a small saucepan over medium heat, then cook until the butter turns deep golden — you'll only need a few minutes for this. Strain to remove any residue (the colour will deepen on standing). Remove from the heat and let cool until lukewarm.

Blitz the almonds in a food processor and until finely ground. Scoop into a bowl and sift the flour and icing sugar into the same bowl.

Put the egg whites in a separate bowl and lightly whisk with a fork until just combined. Add the butter to the flour mixture along with the egg whites. Mix gently with a metal spoon until well combined.

Spoon some batter into ten lightly greased 125 ml (¹/2 cup) friand tins — each friand tin should be filled to three-quarters. Sit the tins on a baking tray and bake in the centre of a 210°C (415°F/Gas 6–7) oven for 10 minutes, then reduce the heat to 180°C (350°F/Gas 4) and bake for 5 more minutes until a skewer comes out clean when stuck in the centre of a friand. Let cool in the tins for 5 minutes before turning out onto a wire rack to cool completely. Dust with icing sugar, then serve. Makes 10.

Made so light and buttery that every crumb melts in the mouth, the friand is the café favourite that makes the humble muffin look positively passé.

Try this luscious sauce over a scoop of ice cream, a warm banana muffin, or a generous slice of caramel pudding.

butterscotch sauce

70 g (2¹/₂ oz) unsalted butter
185 g (1 cup) soft brown sugar
185 ml (³/4 cup) cream

This is a really easy sauce. First, stir the butter, sugar and cream in a small pan over low heat until the butter has melted and the sugar has dissolved. Now simply bring to the boil, reduce the heat and simmer for 2 minutes. Makes 410 ml (1²/3 cups).

A recipe for a good fudge sauce is among a dessert aficionado's most prized possessions.

fudgy chocolate sauce

250 ml (1 cup) cream
30 g (1 oz) unsalted butter
1 tbs golden syrup
200 g (7 oz) dark chocolate, chopped

Put the cream, butter, golden syrup and chopped dark chocolate in a pan. Stir over low heat until melted and smooth and gloriously fudgy and shiny. Serve hot or warm over ice cream.
Makes 500 ml (2 cups).

Eton mess is one of the finer dishes to graduate from the dining hall with honours.

eton mess

250 g (1 punnet) ripe strawberries
2 ready-made meringues
250 ml (1 cup) cream, whipped
to soft, billowy peaks

First of all, hull the strawberries, then cut them into pieces and gently squash the pieces so you're releasing some of the berry flavour.

Now lightly crush up the meringues and set aside. Fold the strawberries and meringue through the cream. Serve in glass dishes — cocktail glasses or old-fashioned sundae glasses are ideal.
Serves 4.

A light and fluffy concoction, perfect at the end of a hot summer's day.

flummery

600 g (1 lb 5 oz) ripe raspberries, crushed
230 g (1 cup) caster (superfine) sugar
2¹/₂ tsp gelatine
cream

Bring the raspberries and sugar to the boil and simmer for a couple of minutes. At the same time, pour 4 tablespoons water into a small bowl. Sprinkle the gelatine on top, then wait for it to become soft and spongy.

Stir your gelatine into the hot raspberry mush to melt it. Now strain through a fine sieve, pour into four glasses and leave to set in the fridge overnight. Serve with lots of cream. Serves 4.

Ever heard of a cookie toll? It's when you bake a batch so good that you just can't pass the cookie jar without stopping for one … or several.

tollhouse cookies

175 g (6 oz) unsalted butter, softened
140 g (3/4 cup) soft brown sugar
110 g (1/2 cup) sugar
2 eggs, lightly beaten
1 tsp vanilla essence
310 g (2 1/2 cups) plain (all-purpose) flour
1 tsp bicarbonate of soda
350 g (2 cups) dark chocolate chips
125 g (1 cup) pecans, roughly chopped

Cream the butter and sugars in a large bowl until light and fluffy — electric beaters make light work of this. Gradually add the eggs, beating well after each addition. Stir in the vanilla, then the sifted flour and bicarbonate of soda until just combined. Now mix in the chocolate chips and pecans.

Drop tablespoons of mixture onto the trays, leaving enough room between them to spread while cooking. Bake the cookies in a 190°C (375°F/Gas 5) oven until lightly golden, about 10 minutes. Cool slightly on the trays before transferring to a wire rack to cool completely, then keep them fresh in an airtight container.
Makes 40.

With its golden, nutty, sticky layers of pastry doused in syrup, baklava is best served with a strong cup of coffee to cut through the sweetness.

baklava

For the syrup:
440 g (2 cups) sugar
2 whole cloves
1 slice of lemon
1/2 teaspoon ground cardamom

235 g (11/2 cups) finely chopped
unblanched almonds
185 g (11/2 cups) finely chopped walnuts
1 teaspoon ground cardamom
1 teaspoon mixed spice
115 g (1/2 cup) caster (superfine) sugar
16 sheets of filo pastry
160 g (2/3 cup) unsalted butter, melted

Start with the syrup — put all the ingredients and 500 ml (2 cups) water in a large pan and bring to the boil. You'll need to stir often to stop it from burning. Simmer for about 10 minutes, then take out the cloves and lemon, and pop the syrup in the fridge to cool.

Grease an 18 x 28 cm (7 x 11 inch) shallow tin. Mix the almonds, walnuts, cardamom, mixed spice and sugar in a bowl. Take 4 sheets of filo and, layering the pastry, brush each sheet with a little melted butter. Fold the sheets in half crossways, trim the edges so the pastry fits the base of the tin, then put in the tin.

Sprinkle one-third of the nut mixture over the filo, then top with another 4 sheets of filo, brushing each with some of the melted butter and then layering, folding and trimming as before.

Repeat the layers twice more. Trim the edges of the top layers of filo, brush with melted butter and score into large diamonds. Bake in a 180°C (350°F/Gas 4) oven until golden and crisp, about half an hour. Now pour the cold syrup over the hot baklava and refrigerate overnight before cutting into diamonds. Serves 10.

index